True Homosexual Experiences
Boyd McDonald and *Straight to Hell*

ALSO BY WILLIAM E. JONES

Is It Really So Strange?
Killed: Rejected Images of the Farm Security Administration
Halsted Plays Himself
Between Artists: Thom Andersen/William E. Jones
Imitation of Christ
Flesh and the Cosmos

True Homosexual Experiences

Boyd McDonald and *Straight to Hell*

William E. Jones

We Heard You Like Books • Los Angeles, California

PUBLISHED BY WE HEARD YOU LIKE BOOKS
A Division of U2603 LLC
5419 Hollywood Blvd, Ste C-231 Los Angeles CA 90027

http://weheardyoulikebooks.com/

Distributed by SCB Distributors

ISBN: 978-0-9964218-1-2

April 2016

First Edition

10 9 8 7 6 5 4 3 2 1

"…one must needs scratch where it itches."
– Robert Burton, *The Anatomy of Melancholy*

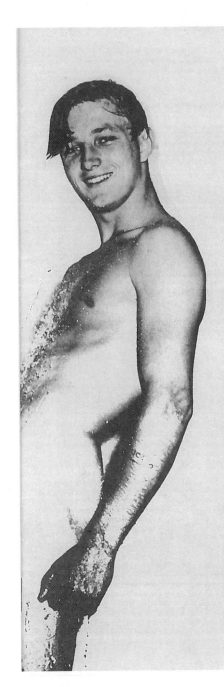

The
Manhattan
Review
of
Unnatural
Acts

NO. 35
BI - MONTHLY
$1.00
MCMLXXVII

Cover of *Straight to Hell* issue 35 (1977).

An Improbably Literate Hustler

Full of anticipation and unsure of what he is looking for, a young man enters an adult bookstore. Stepping through a creaky door bearing a warning sign ("no minors") he heads for the magazine rack. Among the glossy full-color porno magazines giving off a chemical smell, he sees a small, pamphlet-sized publication called *Straight to Hell*. The title recalls condemnations such as "god hates fags," but at the same time suggests defiance—anyone on the straight and narrow path can go to hell. The cover features an image of a naked man who looks nothing like a model, and may be an ex-convict. Not "fabulous" or campy, the booklet seems old-fashioned and homemade, the opposite of what the young man has been led to expect from gay culture. Inside the issue, there is a rhyming slogan in the masthead: "Love and Hate for the American Straight."

Straight to Hell's visual style is immediately recognizable yet anonymous, just like its contents. Lurid, tabloid-style headlines introduce texts contributed by the readers. They describe sex acts between men in many different settings, in various parts of the United States and the rest of the world. This comes as news to the young man: homosexuality is not just confined to a few neighborhoods in big cities and is more or less (for lack of a better word) ordinary. The young man shoplifts a copy of *Straight to Hell*, and at home he masturbates to the words and pictures. Though he doesn't realize it at first, this small booklet has changed his life. On one page, there is an address, a post office box in New York City where he can send orders for more issues and submit his own sex stories. Accompanying the address is a name: Boyd McDonald.

McDonald, founding editor of *Straight to Hell*, was the main creative force behind one of the most distinctive underground publications, in fact, the first queer zine. Self-published and crude, *Straight to Hell*'s sense of urgency was as strong as its contempt for authority. Fanzines and underground comics of the 1960s and early 70s had combined these elements before, but none of them were devoted to homosexual material. From the 1950s onward, early gay publications (e. g., *One*, "The Homosexual Viewpoint" and *Physique Pictorial*) had used the same format—the size of an 8½ by 11 inch sheet of paper folded in half—but none of these prepared readers for *Straight to Hell*. The main difference from its predecessors was its attitude: the man who assembled this material just didn't give a damn about any recognized standard of taste.

Issues of *Straight to Hell* were illustrated with beefcake photographs and candid shots of men. Most were by Bob Mizer of Athletic Model Guild or David Hurles of Old Reliable, but many other photographers and studios were represented: David Alexander, Mike Arlen, Alan Boone, Force One, Kensington Road Studio, Man's Hand, Revolt of Sweden, Sierra Domino (Calvin Craig Anderson), Times Square Studios, and Wavelength. Even documentary photographs by Jack Delano from the Farm Security Administration/Office of War Information Collection at the Library of Congress found their way into Boyd's publications. *Straight to Hell* also published many amateur photos sent in by subscribers.

The unnamed men who contributed their stories came from all walks of life, barely literate to highly educated. Some were young, while others were old enough to remember the early years of the 20th Century. They all had one thing in common: a need to write accounts of their sexual exploits and share them with their fellow men. Boyd McDonald attached great importance to his undertaking; he once wrote, "I consider this history, not pornography. It's very serious work… the true history of homosexual desire and experience. Any gay publications that do not deal with the elemental discussion of gay sexual desire are not serious—they are frivolous." He collected sex stories from a multitude of men and kept his comments on them to a minimum.

Boyd McDonald reserved most of his editorial commentary for news items about the stupidity, hate, and war-mongering of American politicians, and he illustrated them with unflattering photographs. Boyd knew how to spot a con artist, especially one who had wrapped himself in the flag.

Boyd made his political opinions explicit, but he wrote about his personal life reluctantly. A brief account, varying only slightly over the years, became the basis of a compelling biographical myth. One "author's bio" from the early 1980s is typical:

> Boyd McDonald was born in South Dakota in 1925. "I was a pioneer high school dropout," he writes, "leaving school to play badly in a bad traveling dance band. I was drafted into the Army, graduated from Harvard and came to New York, where my principal activity was taking advantage of the city's public sexual recreation facilities. As a sideline I worked as a hack writer at *Time*, *Forbes*, IBM and even more sordid companies…. I started the magazine *STH (Straight to Hell)*, *The Manhattan Review of Unnatural Acts*, later re-named *The New York Review of Cocksucking*."

He describes pillars of the establishment as "sordid" and sends up *The New York Review of Books* by replacing "books" with "cocksucking," a clear statement of priorities. The text is found at the back of the second anthology of "true homosexual experiences" drawn from the pages of *Straight to Hell*. Eventually 13 *STH* collections came out from various publishers. They all had concise, direct titles: *Meat, Flesh, Sex, Cum, Smut, Juice, Wads, Cream, Filth, Skin, Raunch, Lewd, Scum*. A number of proposed titles—*Bare, Heat,*

Hoses, Sex Hounds, Sperm, Stuff, Tools, Used—remained unrealized at the time of Boyd's death in 1993. These books contain descriptions of "how men look, act, walk, talk, dress, undress, taste and smell." At first glance, Boyd's publications might appear to be indistinguishable from the many subsequent ones that copied *Straight to Hell* to less effect and acclaim. A careful reading of *STH* reveals that its editor possessed a unique sensibility; his subversive wit graced every project on which he worked. Boyd had a reputation for being a curmudgeon, and beneath his polite demeanor was a fiercely individualistic anarchist.

IN A RECENT biography, a bit of pleasure reading, I was struck by the phrase "improbably literate hustler," the kind of expression that brings to mind Victorian pieties about a whore with a heart of gold. The writer's assumption, presumably shared by many of his readers, is that for a biography to impart the greatest moral edification, the subject should be respectable (educated and not a whore) or filthy (not educated and a whore). The former kind of subject serves for inspirational stories ("someone just like me has succeeded"); the latter, for cautionary tales ("someone I wouldn't want to be has failed"). The subject who confounds these categories poses difficulties, either when educated and a whore, i. e, unable to act in his or her best interests (a mentally ill person); or not educated and not a whore, i. e., childlike, unyielding, and inscrutable (a saint).

The homosexual, considered mentally ill until fairly recently in the United States, can disturb these comforting habits of mind. The suspicion that educated men were enjoying the company of hustlers when they weren't toiling at their respectable jobs did not occur to the benighted American majority until the latter half of the 1960s, if then. With the arrival of AIDS in the US, an alarming number of homosexuals became physically ill, and the signs were unavoidable: uninhibited fraternizing between men of different ethnic groups and social classes had been taking place, often in public and even in broad daylight, for many years. Then AIDS killed all the really

Paste-up from *The Guide*, the Boston gay magazine. Above: artwork by Keith Haring. Below: Representative Bob Dornan (R-California) worries, and Senator Jesse Helms (R-North Carolina) spits venom.

interesting people, and a group of jealous perverts who appointed themselves defenders of the American way of life unleashed a backlash. Those who came into this world after the worst years of the AIDS crisis may imagine that the moral panic is a thing of the past, like the witch trial, but anyone who lived through that time knows that moral entrepreneurs (when they aren't occupied with stealing money and spending it on hustlers and drugs) are always looking for new excuses to spring into action.

The American puritanism nurturing moral panics also dictates that those with a sexual role in society—prostitutes, pornographers, promiscuous amateurs—cannot be taken seriously as artists. Discounting their work is an example of stereotypical thinking, the mob mentality enforcing conformity. Gay artists who really risked something—usually called erotic artists when not being prosecuted for obscenity, pandering, or endangering children—

have only recently gained some credibility in American culture (e. g., books published and art exhibited). Considering the joyous recklessness of their lives, the erratic quality of medical care for any but the privileged in this country, and that their generation was already decimated by AIDS, they have come to seem like combat veterans, but without medals, because instead of foreign enemies, they have been fighting the prejudice, pettiness, and hypocrisy of American society. They have sacrificed everything so the rest of us can see photographs of naked thugs, experience vicariously the kind of sex sensible people hesitate to seek out, and read stories of their colorful lives in explicit detail. Some of them contributed to *Straight to Hell*; a few are still alive today. They deserve our respect and gratitude.

Almost infantile in its defiance and not acknowledging the boundaries between public and private, *Straight to Hell* is easy to dismiss as the work of an obsessive crank, yet within its pages enduring truths are found. Anyone can see this stuff is trash, but somehow it has never gone away; that is because the social ills *Straight to Hell* diagnoses have never gone away, either. As long as brain and genitals must coexist in the same body, in other words, as long as we are human, we must reckon with Boyd McDonald and his inconvenient messages.

BOYD MCDONALD wrote for most of his adult life, but while he acquired the proper credentials to participate in American literary culture, he ultimately rejected it. Off to one side, he observed the scene with anger and amusement. Boyd read *The New York Review of Books* and placed advertisements in it soliciting submissions to *Straight to Hell*; he read the *New York Times*, but an advertisement he intended for its pages was rejected because it consisted solely of the words "homosexual experiences" and *Straight to Hell*'s address; he wrote for *Time* and *Forbes*, and he later read them with a view to subjecting his former employers to caustic criticism. None of these publications ever mentioned or reviewed Boyd's work during his lifetime, although *Straight to Hell* at the height of its popularity had a circulation of 20,000, and *Meat*, his most successful book, sold over 50,000 copies. Today these figures would qualify any sufficiently presentable writer or editor for literary stardom.

For decades, *Straight to Hell* has attracted a substantial audience while the guardians of official culture have generally remained oblivious. Why this should be the case has a lot to do with the unique path Boyd took in life. He transgressed a number of class boundaries and thereby gained the insights that made his achievement possible. Boyd was born into the Midwestern middle class, educated with the East Coast elite, and worked among New York's professional upper-middle class; in his generation, there was nothing extraordinary about that. Then he had a fall in status, relying on welfare and living in a single room. It was then that his life truly began, and he became the sort of man who deserves a biography. He found a way to thrive in circumstances that would have defeated most people. Boyd used to joke that *Straight to Hell* was the only gay sex magazine funded by the United States Government because he used welfare money to pay his printing bills. Boyd McDonald's work would have harassed the pleasant slumbers of respectable readers had he ever reached them. He did not, and as a result, comfort, complacency, and mainstream recognition eluded him.

Gore Vidal Rests After Reading 'STH'

Vidal first saw STH two years ago; this photo was made within the last two years; thus the caption above is technically accurate, although I can see how its compression of two separate time elements—necessary in a line that brief—might be misleading. In an interview with Steven Abbott and Thom Willenbecher published in *Gay Sunshine* No. 26/27, Vidal evaluated the major media (CBS, *The New York Times, The New York Review of Books,* STH, and so forth). He characterized the last-named as "quite an imaginative little paper, as imaginative as Truman [Capote] when it comes to telling stories about people." Since STH is enchained to Truth, while Capote is free to roam, Vidal's comparison failed to qualify as a money notice. However, I still can't help but admire his *Myron,* for example; I don't permit people's opinions of me to color mine of them. My best friend is presently mad at me, but that doesn't make me mad. I called today and asked if I could visit again providing I'm nice. Thank God she said "tomorrow" (she doesn't have to go to kindergarten tomorrow). But she lives in Boston and I can't make it tomorrow. But our day will come, especially if I give her a certain kind of red shoes she wants. The little whippersnapper.

"Quite an imaginative little paper"—Gore Vidal in *STH* issue 30 (1976).

The
Loved Ones

The biography Boyd McDonald intended for public consumption revealed little. He disclosed a bit more in the "editor's notes" included as asides in *Straight to Hell*. Even with friends, Boyd was very taciturn when it came to personal matters, especially the subject of his family.

After Boyd's death, his sister Dorothy asked Billy Miller, the man to whom he had passed the editorial responsibilities of *Straight to Hell*, "They say Boyd was a homosexual, is that true?" She knew nothing about Boyd as his friends and many readers knew him, yet quite a bit about a family life to which few had access. From Boyd's generation in the McDonald family, those who could confirm a story have died, and even if they still lived, it is doubtful that they could say anything about the Boyd McDonald of *Straight to Hell*. It is unclear what they allowed themselves to know about their relative.

Boyd expressed an aversion to the sort of euphemism that pollutes modern discourse, and he reserved a special hatred for the phrase "loved ones." His expressions of disdain were somewhat ambiguous. He may have been objecting to a pious cliché, or perhaps to the institution of the nuclear family itself, or even to his own family, the locus of conflicts and resentments he preferred to forget; it may well have been all of the above.

Much of what can be learned about Boyd's early life comes from public records and newspapers. His parents, Leo and Ida McDonald, raised three sons and a daughter: Eldon Mark (born 1920); Verle (born 1922); Dorothy Jean (born 1923); and Boyd, the youngest, born in 1925. United States Census reports list Leo as a garage manager in 1930; no profession is listed for Ida. That same year, Huron, South Dakota's local newspaper, *The Daily Plainsman*, carried its first mention of Leo:

> LAKE PRESTON, April 9, 1930—(Special)—Late Saturday evening or early Sunday morning thieves entered the garage of Leo McDonald of Lake Preston and stole about a hundred dollars worth of tires. The cash drawer, which contained only a few pennies, was not touched. As yet local authorities have obtained no clue as to the identity of the thieves.

Almost exactly a year later, there was another robbery, but the victim this time was the man who had leased the McDonald garage only a few days before. The hard times of the Great Depression forced Leo to give up his business and rent the space to another man. The 1940 Census lists Leo as a trucker hauling grain. The Leo McDonald we can discern from these facts conforms to a type: the small business owner and family man who comes down in the world and can no longer be his own boss. It is not farfetched to imagine him drinking heavily; perhaps this was already a problem in 1930, when his garage's cash box contained "only a few pennies."

If the McDonald children were adversely affected by their reduced circumstances, there is no indication of it in the local news. In 1935, two of them appeared in a school play, *Princess Chrysanthemum: A Japanese Operetta in Three Acts* (1905) with words and music by C. King Proctor. Dorothy played the title role, and Boyd, only nine years old, played a villain, Prince So-sli. During the following year, Eldon earned recognition as an excellent student and talented clarinet player. He graduated second in his high school class and enrolled at St. Olaf College in Northfield, Minnesota. While the eldest child was at college, there were more school plays for the younger McDonalds. Boyd also took up the clarinet and won regional high school competitions.

At the beginning of his senior year, Boyd earned his first byline in *The Daily Plainsman*:

Ozarks Haven't Anything On S. D.

By BOYD McDONALD, LAKE PRESTON

September 24, 1942—(Special)—Backwoodsmen are not found exclusively in backwoods districts. One of them told a café waitress, when she handed him a menu, that he could not read and that any dinner she chose to serve him would be OK. He was served a steak dinner, complete with beef-steak sauce. Not able to decipher the word "sauce" on the bottle, he tipped it to his lips and drank it dry. He liked it so much so that he rinsed it, every last drop of it, out with water. After drinking cream out of a cream pitcher, he paid his check and ambled out. The Ozarks haven't anything on South Dakota.

As a youth Boyd began writing short news items for the paper, and his sense of humor was already in evidence. Years later he would include many such items in his columns and books; their subject matter shifted to the failings of politicians, instances of public nudity and sexual activity, and crimes committed within the nuclear family. He would also gain a somewhat different and deeper appreciation for illiterate backwoodsmen.

Boyd described his hometown as a place of "900 souls"—its present population is around 600—and for him as a youth, a city of 10,000 (like Pierre, the capital of South Dakota) was a metropolis. For a while as a teenager, he drove a truck as his father did. Although Boyd later wrote that there were many more "erotic men" in the Dakotas than in big cities like New York or Los Angeles, getting out of the region was a priority for him.

On April 27, 1943, Boyd received one last mention (complete with a jaunty exclamation point) in *The Daily Plainsman*:

> A Lake Preston High School senior has written a song which, according to the song critic of a national magazine, shows promise! The composer's name is Boyd McDonald. The song is called "Got a Post War Plan for My Love."

Shortly afterwards, Boyd skipped town and toured with a dance band that may have been playing his song. This news item describes him as a senior only two weeks before Lake Preston High School held its graduation ceremony and casts doubt on the story Boyd liked to tell about dropping out. His story on the face of it is implausible; Harvard did not as a rule admit high school dropouts. Perhaps Boyd left school as an underclassman then returned to finish his degree, or else he fulfilled all his course requirements then disappeared before picking up his diploma, a gesture that would have made him look like a rebel at little cost.

In *Smut* (1984), Boyd tells the story of having a sexual experience with a man while on tour with his band:

> When I was a teenager, an 18-year-old airman in his blue uniform and I played [a] corny game, both pretending that something that obviously was not true, was. In the lobby of the hotel where I was staying, he invited me to his room for a drink. We had a couple of rye whiskeys and after that the theme of our conversation was that I was too drunk to go home (even though my room was in the same hotel) and that for my own good it would be best if I sleep with him. It was for my own good; my introduction to homosexuality was ideal, at once hot and affectionate, and has given me an attitude that has stuck.

A few months later, Boyd was drafted into the US Army at age 18.

I'll give a little here about the biggest rods I've seen…. One was in the Army. In my barracks in North Carolina there was this little guy from Vermont with a huge hose. At bedtime when we were all stripping he would grab it in his fist and swing it around in great circles. It was so big it didn't look like a dick. It wasn't erotic to him or to me; he and everyone else laughed. His cock was freakish rather than something desirable. He was married and I can't imagine how his wife, or anyone, male or female, could take a prick like that in any hole.

This was Boyd's only published writing about his experience of serving in World War II, and it appeared in *Raunch* (1990).

Boyd made another more general comment about war in an essay written during the George H. W. Bush administration for the Boston gay magazine *The Guide*. He briefly describes the atmosphere of permissiveness—military men looking for (and getting) sex everywhere—that later evaporated with the Cold War anti-gay political reaction.

There has been a dramatic decline in the quality of our wars. Everyone went to World War II because it was a national cause. During World War II, a walk down the streets of a big military base would encounter as many homosexuals as would a walk down the streets of a city with a big homosexual population, like Boulder, Montana (that's right, Montana—but Boulder, Colorado is quite gay too).

Boulder, Montana (population: 1,183) lies halfway between Butte and Helena, and is over 800 miles from Boyd's hometown. He continues,

Since World War II, our wars have been the sort that only heterosexuals do. They were what I call "president's wars." The 45,000 troops who died in Vietnam did not die for our country but for Messrs. Kennedy, Johnson, and Nixon. Little chickenshit adventures have been staged in Grenada for President Reagan and in Panama for President Bush, to say nothing of the toughs they married, Nancy and Babs.

This text was written from the point of view of an old man who had developed political consciousness in the years since his participation in war.

THE VOICE of a teenage Boyd McDonald comes across in a letter he wrote while in the Army. It was addressed to his sister ("Dot") and saved by Merry Laporta, Dorothy's daughter. It bears no date, only "7 p. m. Tuesday." A substantial part of the letter describes a trip to New York and Boyd's companion, a friend with whom he was infatuated.

Dear Dot,

I just returned from New York, where I saw more of New York café society in a few hours than during all the other times together....

Before going any farther, I will explain who I was with. His name is Billy Kober and here are a few facts you can toss together and figure out what kind of a screwy article he is: before he came into the Army, he was the designer for MGM in Hollywood, working with the famous Adrian for $350 a week and $75 an hour overtime; he designed costumes for 17 pictures and his name was on at least one Broadway screen last night; his Hollywood days naturally have netted him personal acquaintants with a mess of celebs.... He has lost (but this seems unbelievable) two sisters, two brothers and his father in the present war; his mother is in London; he was born in Poland and before the war studied in Germany; his wife is a first lieutenant; she was a first sergeant when he married her; he has seen her once. What an article! Oh, yes. He cannot read or write English.

Who was Billy Kober? He did exceedingly demanding but well-paid and desirable work in film production before he was drafted. Adrian designed the dresses of leading ladies, while his assistants designed costumes for supporting actresses and all of the male cast of a film. For an immigrant illiterate in English to have obtained such employment seems almost impossible. The most likely way this could have happened was with the help of a friend or relative in the film industry. The name Kober was not unknown in Hollywood before the war. Arthur Kober (1900–1975) was a screenwriter who (with Dorothy Parker) supplied additional dialogue for Lillian Hellman's film script based on her play *The Little Foxes* (1941). He was also Hellman's ex-husband.

Arthur Kober was born in Brody, Galicia, a city that was part of the Austro-Hungarian Empire before 1919, then part of Poland until the Second World War. It had an overwhelming Jewish majority in its population—at almost 90%, the highest percentage of any Eastern European city—and was among the first targets of the Nazis during the Holocaust. In 1940, a few months after Germany invaded Poland, a concerned mother in London put her son Wilhelm Kober on a boat to the United States. Her concern was justified; almost the entire population of Brody perished by the end of 1942. In his letter, Boyd expresses naïve wonder that so many members of a single family died in the war. As an American enlisted man with no relatives in Europe, he would have known next to nothing about Nazi concentration camps before the US Army liberated Buchenwald in April of 1945.

What sort of relationship Boyd and Billy Kober had can only be guessed from the contents of Boyd's letter. He was excited by Hollywood glamour, but his enthusiastic tone raises a question. Possibly to put a sister's suspicions to rest, he tells Dot that his companion is married (to a woman he has only seen once) and is "quite adept at picking up women." Boyd felt he had gone a little too far, and at the end of the letter he frets about what their mother would think, "I am going to write her a tame version of my latest visit to New York. Don't show her this one. Better burn it. OK?"

Boyd's sister Dorothy, who was closest to him in age, married Richard Shortway in 1945. Before the ceremony, the couple had known each other two-and-a-half weeks. Dorothy's daughter Merry comments on her parents' marriage, "It was indeed a very fast courtship, likely there was pressure, as my Dad was in the Air Force and was being sent away. I bet she felt like she had to wrap it up before he was shipped out, or lose him. [It] would have been better for her if she did let it go; never worked out. She was a country/South Dakota person, not meant for big city or suburban life, and did not deal well with separation from her core family (mostly from her mother)." After the war, Richard Shortway worked as a salesman and he eventually became first an executive at Condé Nast, then the publisher of *Vogue*. Richard and Dorothy lived in New Jersey and had two daughters, Cathy and Merry, whom Boyd would visit regularly. The marriage ended in divorce. Richard Shortway was married three more times; Dorothy did not remarry. She died in 2003.

No trace of Verle McDonald can be found in *The Daily Plainsman* articles from the 1930s, and there is no evidence that Boyd was very close to him. He served in World War II then moved to the West Coast. He lived in Orange County, California, married, and had children. He died in 2006, and his obituary referred to him as a "retired rock and sand processor." He was interred next to his wife Alene and near his father Leo, who spent the end of his life in California.

The eldest child of the family, Eldon Mark McDonald, moved to New York City after serving in World War II like his brothers. At some point, he dropped his first name in favor of his middle name and became an antiques dealer. He never married or had children. Mark McDonald—not to be confused with another Mark McDonald of a younger generation who has very successfully sold "mid-century modern" antiques in New York— specialized in 18th Century furniture. Around 1950, he went into business with a partner, Robert Boerth, a World War II veteran from Michigan. Their shop, Provence Antiques, was at 857 Madison Avenue at 71st Street

BOYD EMMETT McDONALD
Born July 11, 1925 in Lake Preston, South Dakota. Prepared at Lake Preston High School. Home address: Lake Preston, South Dakota. College address: Eliot House. Crimson. Served in U.S. Army. Field of concentration: American History and Literature.

Boyd as a junior at Harvard: "I was completely occupied by my books and papers."

on the Upper East Side, a bastion of conservative wealth and aspiration to such. Provence Antiques was across Madison Avenue from M. Marc, Nancy Reagan's hairdresser, and its phone number was BUtterfield 8-5179, an exchange of special interest to Elizabeth Taylor fans.

Robert Boerth and Mark McDonald also shared an apartment at 155 East 76th Street, a short walk from their shop. They both retired to Connecticut, though they lived in separate towns. Robert died on January 20, 2002. His obituary in the *Hartford Courant* goes into some detail about his life; there is mention of "extensive travel during his lifetime, both for his antiques business and for pleasure," and "an active life of travel, social involvement, and bridge with many close friends," one of whom must have been his former partner. Robert was survived by one relative, a cousin in San Diego. Mark McDonald, who is not listed among the survivors, died less than two months later. His obituary is half the length of Robert's, in keeping with a McDonald family custom of very terse obituaries. The text mentions only Dorothy and Verle McDonald, but not Boyd.

AFTER BOYD'S discharge from the Army, he enrolled at Harvard. In a 1989 video interview, he explained his situation to Jeff Perrotti, a young Harvard alumnus who worked for *The Guide*.

> It was hard to get into Harvard because millions of guys wanted to, but I'd been admitted before the war and given a little scholarship, so I was automatically admitted after the war.... The president of Harvard wanted new blood, and I lived in South Dakota, so he thought I'd be new blood.

Boyd took advantage of his pre-war admission and the G. I. Bill of Rights to get a free education.

Bill Arning, director of Contemporary Arts Museum Houston, never knew Boyd personally, but his father was Boyd's roommate in Eliot House at Harvard. John Arning was close enough to Boyd to ask him to be the best man at his wedding, though the bride and groom were ultimately relieved when there was a last-minute substitution, because Boyd's drinking was a problem and they feared he would ruin the event. When they were students, Bill's father noticed that Boyd had an obsessive quality that expressed itself in pranks such as stealing all the chairs from the dining hall and hiding them in their suite of rooms.

The poet Frank O'Hara, a year younger than Boyd and a Navy veteran, also lived in Eliot House, most of the time with his artist friend Edward Gorey, whose appearance was described by one student as "faggoty." Their circle seemed to be enacting a version of Evelyn Waugh's *Brideshead Revisited* (1945); its elaborate, witty language and emphasis on romantic friendship provided a convenient script for un-athletic boys with a flair for the dramatic. O'Hara, Gorey, and their friends gravitated to the Mandrake Bookstore, which carried Boston's best stock of literature called "camp" or "modernist," depending on whom one asked. Their greatest enthusiasm was for Ronald Firbank (1886–1926) and Ivy Compton-Burnett (1884–1969), whose novels consist mainly of stylized epigrammatic dialogue.

BOYD E. McDONALD
Lake Preston, South Dakota
Lake Preston High School, Lake
   Preston, S. D.
The Crimson
            U. S. Army

Boyd as a senior at Harvard: "absolutely no hint of the sex guru he was to become."

The atmosphere in Eliot House reeked of snobbery, and Boyd, an Army veteran from the Great Plains rather than a scion of the East Coast elite, failed to fit in. If his later work is an indication, Boyd preferred people and literature far less precious than the Mandrake crowd and its books. He went to local bars like the Casablanca and the Silver Dollar with Jim Conant, the son of Harvard's president. The two later worked together at *Time* magazine. As Boyd put it, "We would drink all night."

Boyd studied literature and had an interest in writing. He was on the staff of the *Crimson*, not the *Harvard Advocate*, the literary journal from which alcoholics, Jews, and homosexuals were banned in 1947 at the behest of University trustees fearing scandal, Bolshevism, and sodomy.

Much of the account above derives from Brad Gooch's *City Poet: The Life and Times of Frank O'Hara* (1993) and Douglass Shand-Tucci's *The Crimson Letter: Harvard, Homosexuality, and the Shaping of American Culture* (2003), both histories of great men and very privileged ones. The *Straight to Hell* anthology *Filth* (1987) contains an anonymous story from another point of view. Called "Maid Finds Dirty Underpants in Harvard Bedroom," it was submitted by an alumnus from the same period as Boyd. There is no editor's note accompanying this text, thus no indication of how well (or if) Boyd knew him, nor anything else that would specify the writer's identity.

Of all the benefits I got from Harvard, I am most grateful for the opportunity it gave me, albeit unwittingly, to come out fast and thoroughly.

In the late 40s Harvard developed a large and wild gay subculture. It was right after World War II. Many students were returning to Harvard, or just starting, after their military stint. They were a little older and more experienced than the conventional student and not about to be easily cowed into behaving as school authorities and other conventional people would wish.

There were three houses where most of the gays who were open (to each other—hardly to the University back then) lived: Adams, Eliot, and Dunster. Since I lived in Winthrop, I was not tied in with any of the three circles. I could free-lance and I became involved with all of them.

Late-night parties were frequent. Some guys spread the word that their rooms were open for visitors after the bars closed. (Yes, there were gay bars in Boston even then.) These parties quickly turned into orgies. We were all more or less nice-looking, sexy, high (on alcohol), and ready to fuck the world and each other.

Frequently, these affairs would get a bit noisy, bringing the University police. They were evidently instructed to be polite and respectful since nothing happened other than a mild "Sir, the noise is disturbing those who are trying to sleep. Would you please keep it quiet." Women visitors had to be out of the rooms by 8 p. m. but boys could visit any time.

In my senior year a dean changed this and boys caught in homosexual acts were asked to leave. I escaped being caught—one night literally, by climbing out a second story Wigglesworth window to escape an irate roommate with the University police in tow.

The dean wrote the parents about their sons' outrageous behavior. The father of one boy, a freshman I liked a lot, said to him when he arrived back in the Midwest, "That's it for college. Why don't you get a job in a men's room? Then you can combine business with pleasure."

Parties frequently had a few "straight" boys. Most of the football team one year turned up at some of the orgies. I met my first serious lover at one. It was his first exposure to gay life. He was a freshman, I a senior. He was thoroughly upset by the orgy. He invited me back to his room with the intention (I later learned) of beating me up. Instead we began a torrid affair. I remained friends with him through his marriage (I was best man), 8 children, and lots of lovers of both sexes.

As a 17-year-old freshman, I fell in love toward the end of the year with another 17-year-old freshman in Dunster. I'll call him Teddie.… Teddie thoroughly enjoyed sex so he had to be generous to the University maid, since she'd arrive often enough to find Teddie still in bed with someone. They got along; she accepted Teddie's overnight guests but did scold him once, when she found a very soiled pair of underpants left behind, for sleeping with someone "dirty."

This community of young men having sex with each other in many casual and pleasurable combinations while the authorities looked the other way might seem implausible. After all, these things took place during the "bad old days" when sodomy was still a crime in Massachusetts. The reader can

He gave dick-licking a bad name—Roy Cohn in later years.

decide which description of homosexuality at Harvard in the late-1940s is most trustworthy: an anonymous story from a man who was there, the writings of biographers who seek the truth yet must contend with the wishes of established literary men and their controlling heirs, or the version of history endorsed by a university with a genius for covering up what its administrators and trustees deem scandalous.

One flamboyant young man, G. David Schine in Adams House, was never invited to the orgies. Wealthy and hungry for power, he alienated everyone except his personal valet with his obnoxious demands (a personal secretary to attend class and take notes for him) and awful taste in literature (Ayn Rand). Schine nearly flunked out of Harvard, and his main achievement in writing after graduating in 1949 was a self-published pamphlet entitled "Definition of Communism" (1952), which, in the short space of six pages, "confused Stalin with Trotsky, Marx with Lenin, Alexander Kerensky with Prince Lvov, and fifteenth-century utopianism with twentieth-century Communism," according to Richard Rovere's book, *Senator Joe McCarthy* (1959). *Time* magazine approved of it.

While at Harvard, Schine embodied everything that Boyd would later denounce in his writing. Schine curried favor with twisted old homosexuals while refusing to put out. A woman he dated during his undergraduate days told the *Harvard Crimson* in 1954, "Dave certainly wasn't the type to get involved with a girl," implying that he didn't put out for her, either. Schine was a social climber and would do just about anything to get attention, including getting into bed—politically, if not sexually—with Joseph McCarthy and his chief counsel, Roy Cohn. Gore Vidal expands on this in a 1973 interview with a radical gay Boston publication:

Fag Rag: Getting back to the right wing... the David Schine–Roy Cohn thing is intriguing. We've heard stories of them naked snapping towels in hotels. Did that come out at the time?

Gore Vidal: We used to sing "Come Cohn or Come Schine."
Sure. (Laughter) Senator Flanders of Vermont, noble old boy,
tried to not only knock them off with it but McCarthy himself.

FR: The whole Army–McCarthy hearings were meant as a cover-
up for this homosexual relationship?

GV: Yeah. McCarthy himself was homosexual. This sort of
wing of "perverts."

Boyd's reaction to Vidal's statements about the "wing of perverts" was
this comment in *Straight to Hell*, issue 5 (1973): "Their bitchy and anti-
homosexual homosexuality can only give dick-licking a bad name." After
participating in America's anti-communist hysteria in the most uninformed
and unprincipled way during the early 1950s, Schine took over the family
hotel business. He later got married and fathered six children; he refused to
discuss his political activities or his sexuality with the press.

CHARLES SHIVELY, an editor of *Fag Rag*, stated in an article that Boyd
appeared in 1989 "via video at a protest/celebration—'In Eros Veritas'—
outside the most active Harvard tearoom," the fifth floor men's room of
Lamont Library. This video of Boyd was an excerpt of the interview shot
by Jeff Perrotti on April 3rd of that year. By that time, Boyd's reputation
as a radical gay writer and editor was firmly established, so it comes as a
surprise when Jeff asks Boyd whether he had much sex at Harvard and he
replies, "No. I didn't want any. I was completely occupied by my books and
papers. I really liked being at Harvard. There were some students who hated
it and never cracked a book." If Boyd ever had dalliances with the sort of
unpretentious prep school jocks who never cracked a book and whose images
have spawned generations of menswear advertisements, there is no record of
them. He did little to draw attention to himself. The poet John Ashbery, who
graduated the same year as Boyd and met him when he was visiting Frank

O'Hara in Eliot House, recalls, "I did know Boyd MacDonald at Harvard, but only very slightly. I remember him as rather colorless in appearance and personality, with absolutely no hint of the sex guru he was to become."

Boyd alternated between diligent study and alcoholic binges. The effect on his academic record was mixed. Boyd admitted,

> I took one course in psychology from [behavioral psychologist B. F.] Skinner, which was very difficult for me. I got a D in it, I think, because we weren't allowed to use any of the words that everyone always uses, like love. You couldn't use any word that couldn't be located during an autopsy on a body.

He was much more motivated in his writing courses.

> I had a freshman English composition teacher named Theodore Morrison, who did a book called *Five Kinds of Writing*, which we used as a textbook, and he kept talking in those days, this would be in 1946, mind you, about plain writing. He loved plain writing, the simple, declarative sentence [that you find] in a lot of newspapers. Newspapers are very well written, some of them. Very simple. This is a matter of style. Plain, simple, clear, terse, precise. I didn't know exactly what he meant at the time, but now after all these years, I find that that's what I like, too, and that's what I try to do.

This composition course prepared Boyd for all his subsequent work, first at sordid companies, then with *Straight to Hell*.

BOYD'S CONCENTRATION at Harvard was American History and Literature, and he cannot have failed to encounter one of the leading figures in the field, F. O. Matthiessen, who was Senior Tutor in Eliot House. How

"I look so damned flamboyant"—Walt Whitman's portrait in the first edition of *Leaves of Grass* (1855).

close a relationship professor and student had is uncertain, but it likely had a major effect on Boyd's intellectual formation. Matthiessen's most important book, *American Renaissance: Art and Expression in the Age of Emerson and Whitman* (1941), came to be regarded as a founding text of American Studies.

Walt Whitman's *Leaves of Grass* first appeared in 1855 in a self-published edition not bearing the author's name. Instead an engraved portrait of Whitman faced the title page. The engraving by Samuel Hollyer was based upon a (now lost) 1854 daguerreotype taken by Gabriel Harrison. Whitman wrote about the occasion.

> I was sauntering along the street: the day was hot: I was dressed just as you see me there. A friend of mine… stood at the door of his place looking at the passers-by. He cried out to me at once: "Old man!—old man!—come here: come right up stairs with me this minute"—and when he noticed that I hesitated cried still more emphatically: "Do come: come: I'm dying for something to do." This picture was the result.

To modern eyes, it looks as though Harrison may also have been dying for some*one* to do. The subject of the portrait, long before he was acknowledged as the great American poet, comes across as a casually dressed and rather slutty gay guy. This is no anachronistic hallucination; Whitman in later years had occasion to regret his attitude: "I look so damned flamboyant—as if I was hurling bolts at somebody—full of mad oaths—saying defiantly, 'to hell with you!'" Whitman also said this portrait "was much hatchelled by the fellows at the time—war was waged on it: it passed through a great fire of criticism." His friend William Sloane Kennedy advised "that this repulsive, loaferish portrait, with its sensual mouth, can be dropped from future editions, or be accompanied by other and better ones that show the mature man, and not merely the defiant young revolter of thirty-seven, with a very large chip on his shoulder, no suspenders to his trousers, and his hat very much on one side." Most later editions of *Leaves of Grass* excluded this engraved portrait, and it was supplanted in the public imagination by other images of Whitman, some just as casual but featuring the poet with a long, white beard more appropriate to a distinguished bard.

No less than the author's portrait, the text of the first edition fell victim to second thoughts and revisions, with each edition enlarging and tidying up the original. In later versions all the poems were given titles, and the idiosyncratic poetic lines (much criticized at the time) assumed more conventional forms. Another casualty of subsequent editions was the preface peppered with ellipses, a long text in which Whitman asserts the primacy of the body and sensual experiences.

> As the attributes of the poets of the kosmos concentre in the real body and soul and in the pleasure of things they possess the superiority of genuineness over all fiction and romance. As they emit themselves facts are showered over with light.

Significantly, no matter how famous and established he became, Whitman never expunged the obvious homosexuality of the poems. This moved F. O. Matthiessen to write, "Whitman's language is more earthy because he was aware, in a way that distinguished him not merely from Emerson but from every other writer of the day, of the power of sex."

Boyd placed the following blurb on the back cover of the *Straight to Hell* anthology *Wads* (1985):

> And if Walt Whitman had read *STH*, he would probably have sent us this poem of his:

> I am he that aches with amorous love;
> Does the earth gravitate? Does not all matter, aching, attract all matter?
> So the body of me, to all I meet, or know.

It was an only slightly facetious acknowledgment of Whitman's precedent. Boyd transformed "the superiority of genuineness over all fiction and romance" into a personal motto while editing *Straight to Hell*: "Truth is the biggest turn-on."

For F. O. Matthiessen truth entailed a serious risk, as he himself was homosexual. During most of his adult life he had a partner, the painter Russell Cheney, who was 20 years his senior. Though their relationship was not entirely secret, Matthiessen was careful not to draw attention to it by getting too familiar with the more flamboyant students of literature at Harvard; he was known to cultivate a "straight acting" or heterosexual circle of young men around him. Perhaps membership in this circle was a factor in Boyd maintaining a "colorless" demeanor as an undergraduate, if indeed this was a conscious decision. However wild the undergraduates were behind closed doors, the university curriculum did not acknowledge certain realities. Boyd recalled, "When I was at Harvard, none of the lectures mentioned homosexuality, even when dealing with people like André Gide, Proust, Walt Whitman, and so forth."

Around the time Boyd entered Harvard, Matthiessen was experiencing the most difficult time of his life, due to the death of Cheney in 1945 at age 63. His partner's death deprived Matthiessen of his primary support during bouts of severe depression. He sought to fill the void in his life with political activities, including work for Progressive Party candidate Henry Wallace's presidential campaign. In the new post-war political order, Matthiessen's labor activism (he was, among other things, the president of the Harvard Teachers' Union), his travels in Eastern Europe, and his sexuality made him especially vulnerable, and he was subpoenaed to testify before the House Un-American Activities Committee. On April 4, 1949, *Life* magazine published the unsigned article "Red Visitors Cause Rumpus"; Matthiessen's picture, along with pictures of Lillian Hellman, Langston Hughes, Norman Mailer, Thomas Mann, and Arthur Miller, appears in a section of this article called "Dupes and Fellow Travelers Dress Up Communist Fronts." Although he continued to be prolific in his writing and inspiring in his teaching during the late 1940s, Matthiessen felt himself increasingly under attack and sank into suicidal depression. He killed himself by jumping out a 12th floor window of Boston's Manger Hotel on April 1, 1950.

BOYD GRADUATED from Harvard in June of 1949. He was part of the largest class graduating from four-year colleges and universities the United States had yet seen. People with an interest in such matters expected great things, especially the president of Yale, who called the class of 1949 "one of the finest college classes to come out of Yale University ever." Del Paine, managing editor of *Fortune*, proposed an article, but no one on the staff at that time was interested in writing what seemed certain to turn out as a fatuous puff piece. The assignment went to the new writer at *Fortune*, William H. Whyte, who talked at length to members of the class of 1949, and discovered to his surprise that they were, in a word, dull. Whyte found that things were tough all over. He certainly didn't stumble into any orgies. Perhaps every eccentric of the era went to Harvard. Boyd thought so, and he drew a distinction between his *alma mater* and every other American university, including Yale.

> Going to Harvard gives you the feeling you're really educated because it's such a prestigious university. It gives you confidence. You have to have confidence to do work that is not orthodox. In other words, we had no conformity whatsoever when I was there. It was completely wild and free and I always retained that ever since I picked it up at Harvard. I've done my work with that feeling. I think Yale and so forth have more of an emphasis on conforming. For example, when I was at Harvard, I was glad to be homosexual.... I thought it was extraordinary and heterosexuality was ordinary and I was lucky to be chosen for this minor elite.... At the same time, there was a guy at Yale, who has now become a well known writer here in New York, a playwright and novelist. He tried to kill himself, or he wanted

to kill himself when he began to realize that he was gay. That's not exactly the difference between Yale and Harvard, but there's a little something to it.

Boyd was most likely referring to Larry Kramer (Yale class of 1953) who attempted suicide because he thought he was the only gay student on campus.

Sexuality was not a major topic of William H. Whyte's investigations, but he did notice pervasive conservatism and caution among the students.

This class, at Yale and everywhere else, weren't so hot.... These young people weren't expecting excitement, or challenge. They wanted a safe haven. They wanted to work for AT&T and General Electric, for heaven's sake!

Disengaged from any political questions at a time when sympathies with so-called subversives could cost people their livelihoods, these college seniors also had "little regard for the arts—either as spectators or participants... even for the intellectual of the class the creative role seem[ed] unrewarding."

Over a period of years, Whyte followed this generation in the workforce and transformed his research on the emerging corporate culture of the 1950s into a best-seller, *The Organization Man* (1956). The book described how men of the managerial class looked, acted, walked, talked, and dressed, and the ways they were molded into compliant, disciplined workers with little incentive to innovate and no latitude to express themselves as individuals. The "organization man" made an enormous sacrifice, experiencing a kind of self-annihilation, and all he got in return was a regular job.

AFTER GRADUATION, Boyd McDonald moved to New York and worked as a staff writer for *Time*. In his *New Yorker* article "Omission," John McPhee describes a job Boyd did at the magazine early in his employment there.

At *Time* in the nineteen-fifties, the entry-level job for writers was a column called Miscellany. Filled with one-sentence oddities culled from newspapers and the wire services, Miscellany ran down its third of a page like a ladder, each wee story with its own title—traditionally, and almost invariably, a pun.

For some writers, this sort of column has the attraction of an intellectual puzzle. The master of concision in the genre of short news items (called *faits divers* in French) was anarchist editor and critic Félix Fénéon (1861–1944). He worked for the liberal Paris newspaper *Le Matin* in 1906 and in the space of one year wrote over a thousand such items; they have been collected in English as *Novels in Three Lines* (2007). Fénéon produced an impersonal yet witty running commentary on early 20th Century French society while respecting the strictly mechanical limitations imposed by typography. In addition to these limitations, writers for *Time* in the 1950s had to cope with the magazine's politics.

Time, like *Life* and *Fortune*, was published by Henry Luce. In setting the tone for his magazines, Luce sought editors and writers who were "men of affirmation" rather than "men of protest." Optimism was compulsory in their writing, at least when it came to affirming the values of the Cold War, but the subjective experience of many at Time/Life was anything but optimistic. Several years before Boyd, Walker Evans worked for Luce and managed to publish several portfolios of photographs in *Fortune*. He talked about the experience in an interview from the early 1970s:

> I had to use my wits there. And I think I did all right. I think I won in the long run. I was very pleased with that because that's a hard place to win from. That's a deadly place really, and ghastly. I can't tell you how horrible that is, that organization….
>
> It's insidiously corrupt and its values are a hundred percent the opposite of what any aesthetic or idealistic mind can ever

conceive. But it's hypocritical; they do not admit that. And they play in a horribly dishonest and corrupt way this other game.

In the early 1980s, Boyd told an interviewer how he responded to this environment, "It was such a trauma for me, going to work, that I started drinking that very day. And I drank constantly afterwards."

Writing for *Time* magazine was once known as a springboard to serious literary pursuits, though it must have been known as such chiefly to people who never worked there. As a Harvard alumnus, Frank O'Hara could easily have gotten a job at *Time* and refused; he realized right away that it would have been a dead end. Besides, opportunities at the magazine were severely limited for men of O'Hara's ilk, as Gore Vidal explained:

> A *Time* cover story on Auden was killed when the managing editor of the day was told that Auden was a fag. From 1945 to 1961 *Time* attacked with unusual ferocity everything produced or published by Tennessee Williams. "Fetid swamp" was the phrase most used to describe his work.

Less celebrated than W. H. Auden or Tennessee Williams were (or than Frank O'Hara would later become), but with a mind just as swampy, Boyd might have been a target for fag-baiting "men of affirmation" on the magazine's staff. In his video interview, he described the disadvantage of being a closeted homosexual:

> If you're competing with someone in business, usually they know that you're gay. Quite often they do. He will make all kinds of comments and jokes and things that will be embarrassing. You see, a secret has value. It's something he can use against you, but if you're openly gay, he's got nothing he can do about it.

At that point, being openly gay was not an option, so Boyd had to suffer petty humiliations. He must have realized rather quickly that at heart he was a "man of protest."

BOYD DISMISSED his professional life as a waste—20 years of being a "drunk and hack writer"—and suggested that this was the case from the beginning, but his actual career in journalism was somewhat more complex. A Time/Life in-house bulletin from 1951 provides a few details and gives indications of early promise:

Southern Hospitality

Natchez, Mississippi is a two-newspaper town, where the *Democrat* and the *Times* compete bitterly. The owner-editor of the *Times* is Pulitzer Prizewinner Hodding Carter, a liberal spokesman for the New South who first made his name as the militant editorial antagonist of Huey Long. Carter is considered a hero as well as an astute editor by most good journalists—and *Time* is no exception. This week, it sent *Time* writer Boyd McDonald to satisfy a journalist's dream—to report for Carter's *Natchez Times*. But McDonald will not be leaving *Time*, will merely be taking a six-month leave of absence while he works full hours for Carter....

McDonald came to *Time* from Harvard in the summer of 1949 as part of the year's training program for college graduates. After basic training in the Dallas and Chicago bureaus, he wrote for National Affairs and for the past year has been doing Milestones and Miscellany. On the way to Natchez he will stop off for a week in Greenville, Mississippi, where Carter owns the *Delta Democrat-Times*. McDonald will be able to look over a comfortable situation in the one-newspaper town before plunging into the competitive millstream at Natchez. While he is picking up valuable experience and an intimate knowledge of the South, *Time* will be showing the South its desire to gain a keener insight into an increasingly important region that has traditionally considered itself misunderstood.

Martin Iger
WRITER McDONALD
A journalist's dream.

Boyd in 1951, before his departure for Natchez. The people at *Time* had no idea what this particular journalist was dreaming about.

The articles Boyd wrote for the *Natchez Times* are mainly those of a Northerner gathering impressions in a strange and beautiful place with its own unique customs, and most are not exceptional. There is a story about a penguin laying an egg in captivity; another attests to a professional historian's interest in Natchez.

One article from this period stands out: "House of No Address," published on January 29, 1952.

> The landscape was done, with remarkable restraint, in drab colors. The sky was every shade of gray. With no sun sparkle, the dark Mississippi moved sluggishly and silently. Across the river, Louisiana was a flat brown marsh stretching straight to the horizon without a building or tree in sight. The face of the cliff

was the color of clay, dark evergreen, and leafless winter trees entangled with ropes of fern. On top of the cliff the roofs of houses were all that could be seen of Natchez.

Down here was the other Natchez, the jungle between the river and the cliff. The only sounds were chirping in the brown swamp water and trees creaking in the wind. The old Learned sawmill that takes in logs from river barges had stopped its whining and puffing, since this was Sunday. Since it was also a gloomy Sunday, the darkness and silence of the day gave the jungle beyond the sawmill a prehistoric air.

I followed a path into it. I came upon another clearing and house not seen by those who tour the famous houses of Natchez. Even natives of Natchez are not aware of who lives there. It was a primitive square shack made of odd bits of lumber from the nearby sawmill's discard pile covered over with heavy black tar paper. Washtubs and piles of firewood stood outside. A small window, salvaged from somewhere, took in light. No one was about, but the chickens wandering higher up on the bluff must have a keeper. I decided to return later. I did, and again found no one.

But on my third try, the thin figure of a woman with arms crossed was standing staring at me as I came up the path. She stared, suspicious, inhospitable, unused to visitors, until I came into the clearing and spoke. After hesitating, she said hello too. She was less than middle-aged, scrawny, with tough skin and small faded eyes in her tight face. She had a set expression. She wore a kerchief on her head, and apron over her skirt, and sneakers: her clothes were patched in some places, and needed patching in others.

Before long—although she did not hide her contempt for the idea of being interviewed by a newspaper reporter—she used the occasion to unburden herself. She was bitter but unashamed.

Marion Post Wolcott, *Natchez, Mississippi, August 1940.*

Her name, she said, was Mrs. X. She had had no father since she was three. She had come to Natchez from Texas, with her mother and brothers, when she was eight. She had to work in the cotton mill here. She married, and eleven years ago had a daughter. The father has not been around since then. Two years ago, unable to earn enough money to pay rent in the city itself, she moved down to the rent-free river jungle and set up a house with no address. One of her brothers, a bachelor, already lived in a shack there. With the help of another brother, Mrs. X covered the frame of a shack next door with tar paper, and moved in with her daughter. Mrs. X's mother, 77 years old, lives in a third hut in the clearing. She is the keeper of the chickens.

Mrs. X, when her health permits, earns money washing and ironing clothes for the folks up on the hill. She catches rain water in tubs for washing. The lumber mill provides all the wood she needs. She climbs up the bluff to buy what groceries she can afford. Her church provides groceries occasionally.

It is a life as romantic and old, in its way, as the antebellum mansion life displayed elsewhere in Natchez. Mrs. X's motives are different from those of Thoreau, the great naturalist, but her way of life cannot have changed greatly from Thoreau's way a century ago, when he left the stifling civilization that made everyone lead "lives of quiet desperation," and moved out to a hut on Walden Pond to exist freely, individually, in nature, and off its bounty.

Mrs. X has her own reasons for withdrawing from the ways of the world into a half-world. "Ain't nobody going to bother you down here. I like it; it's quiet. None of those old hanky-tonk radios. No younguns to trouble you. No dogs barking. None of these shows. I don't go to them. I just pray and read the Bible, and try to live right. All I want to do is live right. In these cafés, the waitresses wear paint and flirt with the men to get extra tips. I feel I'm too good for that kind of work. I don't wear paint."

The hopes for their future are uncertain. Mrs. X is not without character: it takes character to live for a week on what most people spend in a day, and there is character in her hard face, and she is not without ambition. "I ain't settled here; I'm not going to spend my life here. As soon as I get back on my feet, I'm going to move back up on the hill." But something besides money seems to be lacking. There is a quality of doom about Mrs. X.

Boyd cared enough about this article to send a clipping of it to his sister. The vivid description of place and character set "House of No Address" apart, but

Marion Post Wolcott, *Natchez, Mississippi, August 1940.*

there is another dimension that lends weight to the story. Boyd saw a bit of himself in Mrs. X. The "quality of doom" and the comparison to Thoreau suggest that through her he gained an understanding of the consequences of nonconformity. Although Boyd undoubtedly felt little sympathy for her severe Christianity, her "bitter but unashamed" resilience in face of poverty and loneliness must have left a lasting impression.

AFTER HAVING BEEN a wallflower at Harvard, Boyd made up for lost time in New York. His corporate day job was a grind, but after work he participated in many sexual adventures, as he explained in his video interview:

The younger gay writers think that there was very little sex in New York until Stonewall… but New York was wildly sexual in the 50s when I came here. The thing is, it was all underground. There [were] Turkish baths, and bars, and men's rooms, and things like that. It was wildly promiscuous. I had sex with a different guy every night, sometimes three strangers in one night…. The 1950s were great for sex in New York. It was just that it was not open.

Boyd once showed Billy Miller the sort of place he could be found during his off hours:

We went to a Greenwich Village coffee place where people used to sit around for hours reading and writing, and he… wanted to stay there long after I was ready to go. He said it reminded him of the 1950s. He also talked about the "Martini Culture" of the 50s and about seeing movie stars and other famous people on the down-low at gay haunts.

One of those famous people was Tennessee Williams:

Boyd told me that Williams would pick up sailors by going up to a bunch of them and just asking straight out, "Who wants a blow job?" and that they'd laugh, but occasionally one or more would take him up on the offer.

It is likely that some of this action transpired in and around the San Remo Café at the corner of Bleecker and MacDougal Streets in Greenwich Village. The clientele included Tennessee Williams, Gore Vidal, William S. Burroughs, among many others, and the place served 15-cent martinis.

BOYD LEFT Time/Life and in 1957 took a job as editorial associate at *Think*, a magazine named after IBM's obvious and condescending motto coined by chairman Thomas J. Watson. *Think* had ambitions to be something more than glossy corporate propaganda, and during the late 1950s, it featured gestures towards Classical learning (an excerpt of Hesiod's *Works and Days*) and critical self-awareness (an article surely intended as a response to *The Organization Man* entitled "Is Individualism Passé?"). Boyd contributed two articles to *Think*: "Electronics Lifts the Iron Curtain," about American electronics engineers observing a Soviet television factory and assessing the USSR's progress in the field; and "New Careers for the Handicapped," about the work of New York's Federation for the Handicapped. The former is a fairly typical expression of the American establishment's Cold War anxiety. The latter, with its descriptions of homebound and bitter people finding hope in joining the workforce, contains passages of real pathos. What this story may have meant to Boyd is difficult to say, but it was his last for the magazine. In the April 1958 issue, his name was dropped from the masthead after less than a year on the staff.

During the ten years between Boyd's departure from *Think* and sobering up, his life story is an almost total blank. By his own account, he continued a transition from journalism to corporate writing. What motivated this change and what disappointments he encountered along the way are uncertain, but it is clear that during this time, he lapsed into serious drinking. He eventually found it hard to hold down a steady job. A friend described the last ten years of Boyd's life in corporate America as "one long bender."

VIRTUALLY THE ONLY reliable testimony we have about Boyd during the lost decade after he left IBM comes from his nieces. In the eyes of children, Boyd was an entirely different person from the one who edited *Straight to Hell*, someone his readers could hardly have recognized. Boyd's niece Cathy Shortway McMullen describes her relationship with her uncles.

Center, second-row from bottom: Boyd's brother Mark with his fraternity brothers at St. Olaf College, 1941.

I saw both Boyd and Mark several times a year as I grew up…. Boyd was a funny, entertaining uncle who really liked my sister and me…. He did not ever divulge what writing topics he was working on to my mother or me. I only learned of his lifestyle after his and my mother's deaths. Mark was a busy and successful antique dealer, also well-educated…. I cannot say what their relationship was.

Boyd revealed nothing about his personal life to the family, but Mark McDonald, on the other hand, was relatively open about his relationship with Robert Boerth.

I was totally aware of Mark's life, knew and liked Bob as an "uncle" as well. We visited them in their apartments several times and they came to New Jersey. Mark had a serious fall while drunk in 1988, and I became his guardian and power of attorney. I had to sell his New York apartment, sell/transfer the antique shop to Bob. I moved Mark first to a nursing home, and he then recovered enough to move to Connecticut until his death in 2002. Bob lived in East Haddam, Connecticut, by then and continued to visit Mark.

Cathy cautiously expands on the topic of alcoholism:

I am reluctant to provide information about the deceased members of my family. Alcoholism was a disease prevalent in the family, possibly in [Boyd's] father, whom I did not know. My mother and Mark were alcoholics who successfully found sobriety, my mother before Boyd and Mark afterward.

The McDonald children took advantage of great social mobility; they propelled themselves far from the modest South Dakota farming community of their origins. What tensions existed between them and what factors contributed to such a high incidence of alcoholism in a single family will probably never be known. It is tempting to look to the short news items that Boyd collected in his columns and books for evidence. Under the rubric "The Joy of Heterosexuality" he summarized and reprinted reports of malodorous bodily functions and felonious parental negligence he considered typical of heterosexuals. Boyd was getting revenge on the mainstream press that selected the most aberrant aspects of homosexual behavior in order to concoct a "typical homosexual" to demonize. Amid *Straight to Hell*'s stories about tearoom sex and adolescent lust, flatulence does not seem entirely out of place, but accounts of abused and neglected children come as a bit of a surprise and disturb the tone of riotous corporeal excess. The texts veer from Rabelais to true crime, with no transition or comment. These items were intended as a rebuke to a heterosexual majority, but they might also have held a more personal significance for Boyd.

While Boyd had no sympathy for negligent parents, their children were a source of delight. Near the end of his last interview, he made a digression which may have struck the readers of *The Guide* (who knew nothing about his family life) as somewhat strange.

> I have an interest—not sexual, mind you—in girls age zero to three.... I see these baby girls at Roy Rogers around the corner where I go for coffee. Their nannies or their mothers bring them in. These little girls take one look at me and they're fascinated, because they can tell in a one second glance that I approve of them, that I find them interesting. It has nothing to do with my homosexuality—well, actually, I think it's a byproduct of it that I should like baby girls and not baby boys. I don't dislike baby boys, but when I'm visiting a place where there is both a baby boy and a baby girl I have to conscientiously do as much for the baby boy as for the baby girl.... Of course the boys can tell I'm just doing my duty.... I'm very good for baby girls that I see in my very limited life.

It is no surprise that the relatives to whom he felt the closest were the nieces he visited from the time they were babies.

Boyd's niece Merry Laporta remembers, "Boyd had such dedicated fun with my sister and me when we were little. He was a weekly, delightful escape from our otherwise careworn lives." She continues:

> I dearly loved my uncle Boyd. Although I did not see him often enough, he was more father to me than my father. This may surprise some people.... We had a loving relationship (albeit restrained; we are, after all, Norwegian as well as Irish). He supported me, stood by me; when the rest of the family called me

crazy, he said I had moxie. I was thrown out of Catholic boarding school for purposely flooding the bathroom after tossing some lightweight furniture out of the window. Both he and I found this rather amusing.

We both appreciated irreverence. I still do, and have him to thank for consistently sharing that with me. He was hilariously funny....

Boyd and Mark (with Bob) used to drive, almost weekly, from New York City to New Jersey when my sister and I were young. (So their rift occurred after we moved from that home in 1959; I don't recall seeing them together after that.) They also came for every holiday and every school "show" until that time. I looked forward to those visits more than anything else in my young life. Boyd always brought candy, ridiculous amounts of it sometimes, but it was not the candy. It was the fact that he actually played with me, took walks, talked with me, took honest interest in my latest stick figure drawing or school worksheet.

Merry fondly remembers Boyd's eccentric table manners, which caused embarrassment and mortification for others. His antic behavior and indifference to convention greatly amused the little girls in his company, and distracted them from unpleasant realities.

Sometimes, we'd go out to eat as a family, a very strained event because of my parents' constant fighting and my mother's more conservative approach to how one should behave in public. Boyd would do things like rearrange all the cutlery so each person had only four spoons or four knives, etc., and/or throw the cloth napkins over his and my food. I remember him saying that the food was too awful to eat, and "you have to cover it with a napkin so the waitress does not see that you left it, or she won't bring you dessert." My mother would try to make him stop, then he'd switch plates or drinks when no one was looking.

There was a radio ad at that time for Robert Hall [menswear retailer, 1937–1977]. They had a jingle, which was:

When the value goes up, up, up,
And the prices go down, down, down,
Robert Hall will show you the reason you go to
High QUAL-I-TY
E-CON-O-MY.

No matter what was happening, when that jingle came on, Boyd grabbed my sister's and my hand and the three of us went up, up, up whatever steps were there, and down, down, down again keeping time with the jingle, in spite of the struggle to turn about in the confined space of a stairwell and do this with any level of grace or coordination. We got quite good at this. It did not matter if we were in the middle of a meal, or at someone else's home for a visit, we acted out that jingle, running to get to the steps in time. It is silly, and one of my fondest early memories. I was three or four.

Merry made trips to see Boyd during the early 1960s:

I used to go into New York City from New Jersey, put on the train by my Mom, at age 10 to 14 likely, and I was otherwise unaccompanied, was then met by uncle Boyd at the train station, at least once a month. All we did was go to the Horn and Hardart Automat for lunch, then he put me back on the train to Jersey.

I LOVED these safe, Boyd-filled trips—five or ten cents into a slot for a tuna sandwich that basically shot out from a metal box, and conversation with a hilarious, loving uncle who insisted, always, that I got chocolate milk and pie.

The psychological problems from which Boyd suffered did not diminish his affection for his nieces, but they made logistics challenging.

> Our future interactions were impacted by Boyd's fight with alcohol first, and then with severe agoraphobia. Years later, when I visited my Mom in New Jersey with the kids, he'd come there by train for literally only two hours. After a few years, he could no longer do that, and I could only see him on his block in the city. This was difficult to arrange. But I understood. He sent letters, I kept only a few, and we had phone conversations. He continued to be very supportive of me throughout my life, and always, always made me laugh. He cared about me and my kids. His queries were genuine, not social niceties. He wanted to gather and hold onto as much info about our lives, their lives, as he could.

Unlike Cathy, Merry was well aware of what Boyd was about and accepted him.

> I am likely the one family member who knew from early on that he was gay, and did not give a shit. I may be the only family who really loved and accepted him, other than my mother. She did love her brothers although she denied their sexuality as much as was possible. Also, I did not know about the scope of his writing, re: sex, until after his passing, and I am not totally comfortable with that, personally, but it changes nothing regarding my feelings for him or my awareness of his absolute brilliance.

> He had more positive impact on my life than anyone else other than a couple of phenomenal teachers who saw in me what I loved in him.

There were limits to what Merry could tell me, especially about her uncle's personal life. "He rarely talked about himself.... I still miss him and wish I had had more contact."

BOYD AND HIS BROTHER Mark stopped seeing each other around 1959. None of Boyd's friends could tell me much about the McDonald brothers' relationship, and neither could Merry:

> I don't know why Boyd and Mark were estranged. Our family was very disconnected, and what's left of it still is, pretty much. Mark and Boyd shared the struggle related to being gay in their era, but nothing else. Mark was... living with a partner (but under the guise of business, for the most part). Some people may have understood the relationship between Mark and his partner Bob; others were likely in that place of denial that is so forgiving and that allows tolerance otherwise denied. Boyd... was radical. They may have simply had the basic political differences, and brotherly jealousies.

Living on opposite sides of Manhattan island—West 70s and East 70s—Boyd and Mark were also at antipodes within the McDonald family. Mark was an academic success and attended a small liberal arts college associated with the Lutheran Church; Boyd affected indifference to academics and even dropped out (whatever that might have meant) but was brilliant enough to graduate from Harvard. Mark visited Boyd at Harvard, and this may have caused friction because he was more popular than a shy, obsessive, "colorless" Boyd—and possibly more welcome at the Eliot House orgies described in *Straight to Hell*. Eventually, differences in the politics of how they chose to lead their lives caused the two brothers to part company.

BOYD OFTEN MADE the remark that heterosexuality was a socially conditioned choice, like living on the East Side, and he poured scorn on the bourgeois homosexuals who facilitated the overblown, imperial lifestyle of the Reagans: hairdressers, dress designers, decorators, and antiques dealers. With them in mind, Boyd wrote a screed called "Wax Fruit," published in issue 48 (1980) of *Straight to Hell*:

> I write for the lower and upper classes, not the Rising Middle Class. *STH* is always coarse, never common; the middle class are endlessly vulgar, with no redeeming obscenity.... They represent themselves as above sex, but... they are beneath it—too cold, too frightened, too ambitious, too conventional, too unattractive for sex.... To this day they love lovely things. They are themselves lovely things, things more than people, robots like the "straights," performing as programmed by the "straight" world and, in their case, the Gay Liberation Movement. They are the sort of "gays" their mothers always wanted, but no one else does; they are the true undesirables, the undesiring.

For Boyd, the only ethical alternative to the frigid hell he described was downward mobility, identification with the poor, and membership among their ranks, which was not a normal choice in the grasping 1980s, and certainly not the one made by his brother.

MARK MCDONALD'S side of the argument has little to support it now that he is gone. His one published piece of writing was a letter to the *New York Times* in response to a Sports Section editorial about gender stereotypes and athletics. The writer, Dan Wakefield, describes an unnamed celebrity failing miserably to make a shot on the basketball court. A spectator says, "Einstein probably couldn't make a lay-up either." The writer continues,

It seems a simple observation, and yet it is not one that comes easily in a society that brainwashes males with the notion that "manhood" is equivalent to athletic prowess....

I sincerely look forward to the time when Dick and Jane can run and jump and sew and read and paint pictures according to their inclinations and talents rather than to the arbitrary rules of their respective sexual roles as dictated by society.

See Dick bake a cake! See Jane knock a homer! Hurray for Dick and Jane!

On May 25, 1975, the *Times* printed a response from Mark, "Don't Judge Talent Merely by Sex":

To the Sports Editor:

A big cheer for Dan Wakefield ("All Boys Aren't Athletes, and Some Survive," May 11). It's about time that those skills, athletic and otherwise, that are valued by our society were liberated from the genetic connotations that have afflicted them in the past.

But I would also like to throw a small Bronx cheer Mr. Wakefield's way. As Thomas Jefferson observed some time ago, long before the advent of professional sports and even sandlot baseball, "There is a natural aristocracy among men."

Unfortunately, chauvinist that he was, Jefferson failed to include "and women" or delete "men" for "persons." But his idea that each of us is unique by virtue of our own particular skills and talents is obvious; his point then was that some men were more fit to govern than others. Let's preserve some variety, that aristocracy of talents.

Mr. Wakefield's point is obvious, too, and noble. Indeed: Sew, Dick, sew; Slide, Jane, slide. But also: Dunk, Kareem, dunk.

Mark McDonald
New York City

The letter above raises the question of what the two McDonald brothers had in common; there is a certain similarity in their writing styles. Boyd would not have invoked a concept like "natural aristocracy" in reference to American society, though he might have used the phrase to describe the sexual prowess of some American men. The brothers also took an interest in similar subject matter. In issues 5 (1973) and 7 (1974) of *Straight to Hell*, published before Mark's letter and near the end of the Vietnam War, Boyd takes aim at unthinking gender stereotypes as they were propagated by his former employer:

> [*Time* magazine's] latest jackoff fantasy concerns a psychiatrist in lower California who gives therapy to "girlish boys" in hopes of "butchering"—making more butch—their sensitivity, so that they can get out and play ball with the boys, indulge in competitive name-calling, and enter the virility rat race like everybody else. If *Time* magazine and its new hero, Dr. Green, could have their way, today's budding Shakespeares and Einsteins would drop those sissy books and join the Little League, which is what really matters. "Left untreated," *Time* warns, "most of them would grow up to be homosexuals." Left untreated, many other boys grow up to bomb hospitals and orphanages in Southeast Asia, shove entrenchment tools up Vietnamese vaginas, bait "fags" on TV while aggressively looking for cock off-camera, peddle justice to the highest bidder in the Nixon administration, become sex-crazed cops who seduce homosexuals in shit houses and mug them when they accept....

Dr. Green urges parents of "sissies" to deny them TV privileges as punishment for "effeminate" behavior. But how the fuck else can they learn to dress like cowboys, jocks, bombers, and hoods?

Compared to Boyd's self-published rant, Mark's letter published in the *New York Times* comes across as mild-mannered, even a bit prissy. If this contrast in tone existed in conversations between the brothers during the 1950s, it is easy to understand how uncomfortable a weekly car ride to New Jersey must have been for them.

None of the McDonalds were known to have played sports, but based on his reference to Kareem Abdul-Jabbar, one of the NBA's all-time greatest players, Mark seemed to prefer basketball, as perhaps Boyd also did, if the following contribution to issue 47 (1980) of *Straight to Hell* can be accepted as evidence:

From a reader—I'm enclosing photos of my closest high school buddies, dating from the late 50s. They were my steadiest sex partners, although like the many others I blew, they always asked me not to tell. I never did tell, but I never asked the same of them.

Consequently I had lots of referrals. #31 was my first regular (about once a week). We started in about the third or fourth grade. He never reciprocated in kind but after I ate him would often roll over to get fucked. I imagine his older brother, whom I once serviced and who had the biggest tool in town, must have initiated him.... My best friend in youth was #5. I don't think anyone but one person ever suspected what we did. We did it two or three times a week until our junior or senior year.... #5 and I did everything together—camped out together, studied together, played with each other....

In our junior or senior year he gently told me he couldn't do it with me anymore (I think under pressure from his then girl, now wife, who knew).... He's now the superintendent of schools in

The fellated: numbers 31, 5, and 25.

the town where he grew up and has two kids. #25... was a really hot number who needed it almost every day, if not twice daily. I guess #31 probably told him about me because one steamy summer night in a vacant lot he just pulled it out and shoved my head down on it. He especially dug doing it in houses being built or at the steering wheel.... He did not often reciprocate but occasionally took me down his throat and always let me come on his leg. So far as I know he is still a gas station man in my hometown.

It would be going too far to assert that this story took place in Lake Preston, South Dakota, but the atmosphere of high school athletics and the libidinous pasts of a school superintendent and a gas station man do suggest the small-town life of the Great Plains.

In an earlier *STH* article, Boyd conducted a detailed interview with a former trucker who had had sex with over 700 men while on long hauls. He categorized his sexual experiences with fellow truckers:

Are there "types"—that is, types of truckers that prefer one kind of sex? Definitely, although in every line of trucking there's always those who will do anything. But bullhaulers, for example, are generally out to fuck you. A bullhauler is a cattle truck driver. They love to fuck a guy's hole raw so if you can't handle it don't try it. Tank drivers generally like to suck or get sucked. Tanks are liquid—gasoline or milk. Milk runners aren't usually too good because they're mostly local runs and the guys don't get hot enough, but I've met some who are good. The long-distance gasoline drivers are good. They're the best cocksuckers and they love having their cocks gobbled. Produce haulers are usually anal, for some reason. They love being packed in the ass.

What did you like best? Mixing it up—all of it. Like a tank hauler in the morning, eating and being eaten, around noon maybe a piece of ass from a produce hauler, and then that night, getting my own hole fucked raw by some bullhauler. I used to love the smell of their sweat as they fucked me. It was really masculine. Really a turn on.

Was there much sex at truck stops where drivers spend the night? Not too much. But we'd exchange truck numbers so that you could get a good cocksucker or a good piece of ass when you recognized his truck.

What kind of guys are long-haul movers—you know, furniture? They're really way out. A lot of chicken hawks among them. I knew one guy used to take his own 13-year-old son with him on runs during the kid's summer vacation so that the kid could attract other boys at rest areas. His dad would suck the kids off. One truck was pretty notorious—the entire crew was chicken-oriented. They sucked every kid they could get their mouths on along the way. They also liked groups—sucking and fucking with a bunch of young boys.

Would you say most long-distance movers are chicken hawks? No, but a lot of them. But they are way out. The first time a guy ever drank my piss, he was a furniture hauler.

This is by far the longest article in the issue (number 20, 1975). The topic may have held a special interest for Boyd, because he and his father worked as truckers. Boyd never asked his informant what particular kind of sex grain haulers prefer; perhaps he didn't need to. He often referred to the "erotic men" living outside major metropolitan areas in the US, and it's possible that his brief teenage employment as a trucker in South Dakota provided him with experience of them.

BOYD FELT much greater rapport with the women in his family than with the men. He encouraged his nieces to assert themselves and not to submit to mindless conformism. He appreciated evidence of his anarchic spirit in younger generations. In every letter, he sent money so the children could have extra toys and candy, even when he could ill afford the expense.

Merry Laporta has saved an important letter from her uncle dating from 1967. Boyd wrote it by hand and gave her a new address, 5 West 63rd Street. Although the letter does not acknowledge it directly, there are indications that Boyd had fallen on hard times: he must have lost or pawned his typewriter, and the place to which he had moved was the YMCA.

In the letter Boyd urges Merry to do one big thing to placate her elders: to get a college education. She had been dissatisfied with her freshman year and was considering dropping out; Boyd suggests staying a while longer and transferring to another college. He tells her he approves of the changes taking place in America during the 1960s, and he believes staying in college would afford her the best opportunity to play a part in them, even if that entails

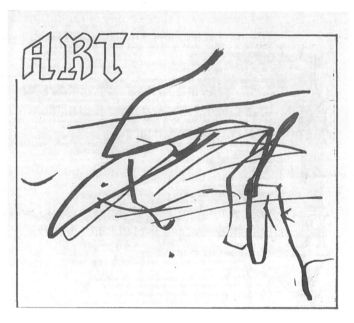

"Brazenly authoritative slashes" by Boyd's great-niece Suzanne.

burning down the school. Boyd expresses complete faith in her abilities, and this message must have meant a lot to his niece, because she stayed in school.

Merry later raised two daughters with whom Boyd had close relationships. One of them, Suzanne, features improbably in issue 13 (1974) of *Straight to Hell*.

> This line drawing is a gift from the artist. I have known her all her life—and known her well. She lets people know her well, even inviting them to watch her go to sleep or take a bath. There are six toy animals in the tub (seven counting her).
>
> She is Suzanne Supergirl, beautiful and tough, and sweet beyond belief. She is four now. She tells me she dreams and wonders if I do too.

She dashed this line drawing off in a few inspired seconds. While running from the living room to the kitchen she noticed her drawing paper on the dining room table, paused just to execute these brazenly authoritative slashes, then ran on to the kitchen for a pit stop (grape juice)....

What is she doing in a paper like this? Well, she likes people who like her and does not readily submit to unreasonable restraint; when someone suggests she quiet down she says (as though it were relevant, and I'm afraid it is), "I don't *want* to quiet down." What could be more appropriate?

It's just appalling, how interesting she is.

Ever the indulgent uncle, Boyd referred to Suzanne in letters as The Angel.

THE ONE WOMAN missing from family memories is the matriarch, Ida McDonald. She looms in the background undescribed and silent. There is no mention of her in the various news items from *The Daily Plainsman*. According to his friends, Boyd said only a few things about his mother, and all of them were laced with irony. In a letter written to his friend Jim Tamulis in the early 1980s, Boyd gives a reason for taking his distance from the family:

Intelligence brings self-confidence, and intelligent people can afford to like what they like without caring... what their mothers would think. No one is fonder of mothers than I, but I don't think they ought to be editors of our work. In fact, if our work is any good, I don't think they ought even to see it.

In his video interview, Boyd explained further when Jeff Perrotti asked how his family reacted to the work he was doing.

Family reunion: the McDonald grave in Lake Preston, South Dakota.

They don't know about it. Somebody asked me, "How can you do this kind of work?," and I said, "Because my mother died." You can't integrate this kind of work with your family, but there's no reason why you should. You don't want to hear about your parents' or brothers' and sisters' sex lives, and you wouldn't tell them about your own, except that you were gay, but that's an abstract term: gay. My work is homosexual, which is specific, concrete, detailed. It's nothing to say that you're gay. Your parents can handle that, but it's when you go into the details that it becomes difficult. I wouldn't want my family to see any of my work.

Considering statements from his niece Cathy about how little she and her mother knew of Boyd's personal life, he must have been as successful as he could have hoped in keeping his mother in South Dakota from seeing anything disturbing. The question still had a lingering importance for Boyd; his letter to Jim Tamulis dates from 30 years (and the video interview nearly 40 years) after his mother's death.

Ida McDonald died in 1950, a year after Boyd graduated from Harvard and long before he started *Straight to Hell*. At that point, he was working for *Time* magazine. There appears to have been no problem or scandal there, at least from his employer's point of view. Earlier at Harvard, Boyd did not pursue sex, and it is doubtful that word of any homosexual activity reached his family. It seems likely that there never was a scandal, only a censorious presence haunting Boyd's thoughts. And not only Boyd's—as adults, all of Ida's children moved as far as possible from the family home; it may have been a stern maternal figure who drove them away.

Boyd's mention of "the sort of 'gays' their mothers always wanted" in "Wax Fruit" raises the question of sibling rivalry developing over decades. Who was Ida McDonald's favorite, Mark the first-born or Boyd the baby of the family? We will never know; perhaps the McDonald sons themselves never knew.

Boyd's alienation from his mother extended until his death. The volumes of Boyd's published and unpublished writing contain only the slightest references to her. There was no reconciling this separation, and yet, a reunion of sorts did finally occur. The three unmarried McDonald children—Mark, Dorothy, and Boyd—were buried in the family plot in Lake Preston, South Dakota, together with their mother, Ida.

Cover of *Straight to Hell* issue 20 (1975).

The Ivy League Fuck-Up

In 1968, at the end of one last bender, Boyd McDonald found himself on Long Island, where he did not live and had no family. He checked into the Central Islip Psychiatric Hospital to "dry out," and the treatment worked. He explained to Jeff Perrotti, "I had DTs for a week, *delirium tremens* where you see fantasies, so they had [me] strapped down by [my] ankles and wrists…. It took a week and I've been out of it ever since." Boyd was 43 years old. During the period leading up to his time in the hospital, he had lost the last in a succession of jobs he held after leaving IBM, his apartment, and almost all of his possessions. Upon his release, he carried out everything he owned in a shopping bag. Summing up his experience, Boyd often repeated the following story:

> I took my suits to the pawnshop. In those days there were pawnshops where you could take clothing. It was like burning the mortgage: I remember the feeling of exhilaration when I realized I couldn't have gone back into an office as a writer even if I'd wanted to.

61

He applied for welfare and found a place to live in an SRO (single room occupancy) hotel, the only accommodation he could afford and a place where he could live quietly and anonymously.

Boyd cut ties to his former life, except to the family he would see less and less frequently. He was off the map; the 25th Harvard Class Reunion Report for the Class of 1949 listed him as "lost." The people from the alumni association didn't trouble themselves to look for him. He had no money to contribute to their fundraising appeals anyway.

Stephen Greco, who interviewed Boyd for the *Advocate* (the gay magazine, not the Harvard literary journal) and later became a good friend, describes Boyd's "inherited privilege" as a young, white Harvard graduate who "eagerly cultivated noncompliance":

> He was among "the best little boys in the world," [and] there was a certain role for a well-educated, decorous gay man who could do tricks of thought. If you did the right tricks, you gained power in the media. You also validated values that may or not may be in your larger interest. I choose the word "noncompliance" because I think he was very aware of stepping away from something. He wasn't just a druggie dropout. He wasn't a randomly angry revolutionary. He decided to not comply with the system that he knew didn't describe a life he recognized.

Boyd landed at a level of society below the bohemia where middle class kids rebel and hide out for a while; it was a place from which he could not easily escape.

THE SAME YEAR that Boyd "dropped out," Gore Vidal published his satirical novel *Myra Breckinridge* (1968), which was denounced as obscene by some conservatives, and consequently became enormously popular. In the following passage, the title character, having searched the medical records of the students at her Uncle Clem's Hollywood acting school, reflects upon the penis:

> Just as I expected, seventy-two per cent of the male students are circumcised. At Clem's party I had been reminded of the promiscuous way in which American doctors circumcise males in childhood, a practice I highly disapprove of, agreeing with that publisher who is forever advertising in the *New York Times Book Review* a work which proves that circumcision is necessary for only a very few men. For the rest, it constitutes, in the advertiser's phrase, "a rape of the penis." Until the Forties, only the upper or educated classes were circumcised in America. The real people were spared this humiliation. But during the affluent postwar years the operation became standard procedure, making money for doctors as well as allowing the American mother to mutilate her son in order that he might never forget her early power over him. Today only the poor Boston Irish, the Midwestern Poles and the Appalachian Southerners can be counted upon to be complete. Myron never forgave Gertrude for her circumcision of him. In fact, he once denounced her in my presence for it. She defended herself by saying that the doctor had recommended it on hygienic grounds—which of course does not hold water since most foreskins are easily manipulated and kept clean. What is truly sinister is the fact that with the foreskin's removal, up to fifty per cent of sensation in the glans penis is reduced... a condition no doubt as pleasing to the puritan American mother as it is to her co-conspirator, the puritan Jewish doctor who delights in being able to mutilate the *goyim* in the same vivid way that his religion (and mother!) mutilated him. I once had the subject out with Dr. Montag, who granted me every single point and yet, finally, turned dentist and confessed, "Whenever I hear the word 'smegma,' I become physically ill." I am sure Moses is

roasting in hell, along with Jesus, Saint Paul, and Gertrude Percey Breckinridge. I was not able to find Rusty's medical report and so do not know whether or not he has been circumcised. I hope not for I prefer the penis intact… in order that it be raped not by impersonal surgery but by me!

In an unpublished article about the beginnings of *STH*, Jim Tamulis recounts the effect the book had on Boyd:

> It was this passage in… *Myra Breckinridge* that sent Boyd McDonald straight to hell. It was his first awareness that others besides him took special interest in the cut or uncut disposition of the cock. This prompted him to advertise in the *Advocate* that he was on the lookout for likeminded men. The response was encouraging, and he began circulating through ads in the sex papers his own mimeographed newspaper, *Skinheads*. Besides putting these likeminded men in touch with each other, it ran accounts of the sex lives and desires of its readers, which came in unsolicited. Frustrated or insatiable men were evidently grateful to find a sympathetic ear. They let it pour out.
>
> McDonald—Harvard grad, ex-GI, recently sobered-up alcoholic—had nothing in his life except occasional assignments from Office Temp, and he got the idea—based on the responses to *Skinheads*—to start publishing and writing his own I. F. Stone newsletter of sex, *Straight to Hell: The New York Review of Unnatural Acts*.

It was clear from the beginning that Boyd had found his calling.

STRAIGHT TO HELL did not burst forth fully realized. After he was inspired by *Myra Breckinridge*, it Boyd took a few years to produce his first issue, which must have had a very limited circulation. The earliest copy of *STH* I have been able to see is issue 3 (1973). My initial reaction was one of shock; there is no other way to describe it. I had been accustomed to the look and content of issues from the 1990s (when I discovered *STH*) to the present; these are relatively clean, designed on computers, well printed, and consonant with what readers have come to expect from a queer zine. By comparison, the early *Straight to Hell* issues are beyond the pale. With the production values of old mimeographed newsletters circulated among high school students and their parents, they are completely at variance with acceptable discourse as understood by mom and pop. There is something in them to offend the whole family. The first page of issue 3 features a barely legible image of a guy flashing his cock, typewritten text, and amateurishly handwritten headlines like "Sailor Sucks Off 3 GIs" and "America's Sexual Nazis." The latter story is illustrated with the boldest graphic on the page: a swastika.

Swastikas appear in *Straight to Hell*'s first 31 numbers, published 1973–1976. In issue 10, Boyd explains their presence:

> Several readers have asked about the swastika. It should be obvious, but obviously isn't, that the swastika is a symbol of what I'm against not what I am for. America is a sexual dictatorship and the "Master Sex" brutally enforces heterosexuality. Anyone in the police, media, the church, the streets who has some reason for wanting to seem "straight" can use this atmosphere to bait, bully, beat, and boast. The insistence on heterosexuality raises obvious questions: If it's so natural why does it have to be enforced? If it's so satisfying why are "straights" so jealous of homosexuals? If "straights" really are straight why are they so anxious to show it? The Nazis at least had the erotic "blond beast" type. We have sick cops, sickly male impersonators like Dick Cavett, greasy male sluts like Dean Martin, senior male bitches like Bob Hope.

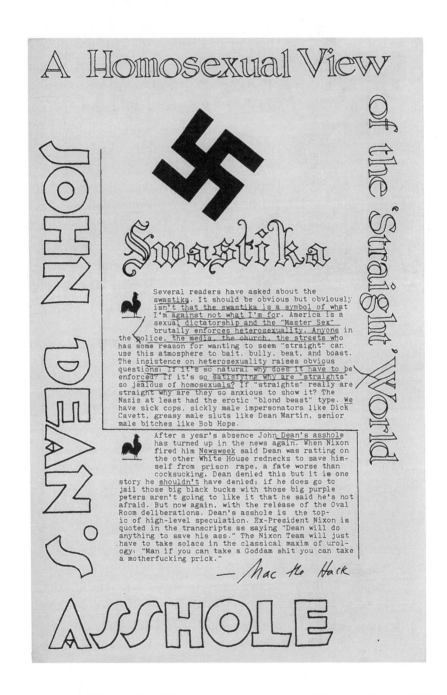

A Homosexual View

of the 'Straight' World

JOHN DEAN'S

ASSHOLE

Swastika

Several readers have asked about the swastika. It should be obvious but obviously isn't that the swastika is a symbol of what I'm against not what I'm for. America is a sexual dictatorship and the "Master Sex" brutally enforces heterosexuality. Anyone in the police, the media, the church, the streets who has some reason for wanting to seem "straight" can use this atmosphere to bait, bully, beat, and boast. The insistence on heterosexuality raises obvious questions: If it's so natural why does it have to be enforced? If it's so satisfying why are "straights" so jealous of homosexuals? If "straights" really are straight why are they so anxious to show it? The Nazis at least had the erotic "blond beast" type. We have sick cops, sickly male impersonators like Dick Cavett, greasy male sluts like Dean Martin, senior male bitches like Bob Hope.

After a year's absence John Dean's asshole has turned up in the news again. When Nixon fired him Newsweek said Dean was ratting on the other White House rednecks to save himself from prison rape, a fate worse than cocksucking. Dean denied this but it is one story he shouldn't have denied; if he does go to jail those big black bucks with those big purple peters aren't going to like it that he said he's not afraid. But now again, with the release of the Oval Room deliberations, Dean's asshole is the topic of high-level speculation. Ex-President Nixon is quoted in the transcripts as saying "Dean will do anything to save his ass." The Nixon Team will just have to take solace in the classical maxim of urology: "Man if you can take a Goddam shit you can take a motherfucking prick."

— Mac the Hack

Boyd McDonald ("Mac the Hack") explains his frequent use of the swastika and "high-level speculation" about a Watergate conspirator's asshole. (Text has been underlined by a subscriber.)

Boyd used the swastika to point out examples of fascism: multiple stories taking place in Vietnam (where the war was still going on); an interview with "dirt" (a vice squad officer); a photo of Pope Paul VI taken when he was a Vatican official during the fascist era. A swastika dots the letter "I" in most titles containing the word "straight" in early *STH* issues.

Current *Straight to Hell* editor Billy Miller gives his opinion about the preponderance of swastikas: "Boyd wasn't in any sense fascist/racist/anti-Semitic but used that… for its power to get attention. It's about irony and Boyd's dark humor. He was 'punk' before punk, among other things." Around the time the word "punk" gained currency outside the prison system (and the pages of a New York music fanzine), Boyd stopped using the symbol. Billy adds, "As far as why swastikas disappeared from *STH* later in the 70s, that has everything to do with changes in distribution and how/where the publication was marketed/sold." The shock value of the swastika had worn off a bit once it became a fashion statement, and as *STH*'s circulation increased, it became a hindrance prone to misunderstanding.

Early *Straight to Hell* has all the indications of a deeply personal tirade addressed to a select audience. Boyd spent years writing for mass market publications where every word was subjected to scrutiny and made to conform to rules, i. e., financial and ideological constraints, especially at Time/Life. When he left a corporate environment, the flood gates opened. His literary skills did not abandon him, but his sense of shame certainly did.

By the end of the 1970s, *Straight to Hell*'s production values improved; issues featured offset printing, halftone photo reproduction, and stapled (as opposed to folded and gathered) pages. Periodically, the masthead contained circulation figures: 2000 (1975); 4000 (1977); 8000 (1979); in the 1980s, under the editorship of Victor Weaver, circulation reached 20,000. Boyd originally called *Straight to Hell* a "newsletter for us," but in the space of a few years, his publication reached an audience well beyond the small group of original subscribers.

RAUNCH & RADICALISM

The Amazing
STRAIGHT TO HELL
No. 14 MCMLXXIV

The New York
    Review of
    Cocksucking

The American
    Journal of
    Revenge
    Therapy

Sperm Illustrated

The Rimmer's
    Digest

The Saturday
    Evening
    Ass-Licker

Sex-Pol

G.I.
    (Gender Identity)
    ****

"Love and Hate
    for the
    American
    Straight"

"America's Best-
    Loved Journal
    of Dick-
    Licking"

"The Paper That
    Made New
    York Famous"

"Alone In Its
    Greatness"

"The Truth--
    No Shit"
    ****

Pro Homosexual

Pro Women

Pro Children

Anti "Straight"
    ****

60¢ the Copy
12 Issues, $6
Europe: $7
Checks to Cash

AMG

Box 982
Radio City Station
New York City 10019

Please do not use STH in address

Straight to Hell issue 14 (1974): its masthead contained a long list of alternate titles.

A MUSCLE QUEEN IN THE WHITE HOUSE

He golfs, he swims, he jumps the trampoline: he's your President and mine, Jerry Ford. He often eats only an English muffin for breakfast and cottage cheese for lunch. He called in photographers to take just-plain-folks pictures of him preparing his own breakfast--that is, toasting his own muffin. It's so hard to get de-

cent help these days, even in the White House; who remembers a decent President?

He's worried, he said on national TV, about his waistline. To do all that exercise and eat so little and still have a gut like that is merely disgusting; to worry about it more than he worries about equal justice is depraved.

"Merely disgusting"—on the facing page Boyd makes his characteristic political commentary.

ALTHOUGH *STRAIGHT TO HELL* was available in adult bookstores, Boyd made a crucial distinction between his work and the fantasies sold by commercial pornographers.

> The thing that all my work has in common is that the truth is more pornographic than pornography. These things in my books not only can happen, but did happen. It's more exciting that something did happen, rather than some lone fiction writer imagines that it happens.

In editing stories for *Straight to Hell*, Boyd never lost sight of the importance of retaining the "boring" parts, because

> that makes them sound like authentic documents. There's a guy in West Virginia who will write that he works at a hardware store and… a few comments about Reagan and so forth, and I try to leave that type of thing in because it makes it sound like real people rather than hack writers. Any hack writer can be coherent, but these are amateur writers and they put a lot of incoherent things in…. The letters I like are the ones that are pretty ragged. A lot of fears and flaws, failures. The three Fs…. Some of the guys try to organize them and make them quirkier and have little punch lines at the end. Little neat, O. Henry type stories…. I don't like them organized. I like them to sound as though they were talking to you.

Boyd made pragmatic and subversive comments on the difference between what is pornography and what is not. He sets out a program in his essay, "Art from the Post-Heterosexual Age" (1986):

> Many artists escape the restrictions of the media and do the work they want to do simply by calling it something other than what it is. It is best, for example, to call sexual writing sociology.

People, bless them, are at least sometimes willing to let you define yourself and your work and willing to believe you are what you say you are and your work is what you say it is. The best policy is to establish abruptly, tersely, and immediately at the very beginning, that your work is art.

Boyd, who had established himself tersely at the very beginning of his endeavor, implies with this statement that his own work is art and that he is an artist. Some would disagree with him, because *Straight to Hell* was originally sold in places that were less than respectable, Boyd's sources were usually anonymous, and the photographs he used to illustrate his publications left little to the imagination. As Boyd would have been quick to point out, this judgment is based upon class distinctions that do not properly pertain to whether something is art or not. His practice of editing and arranging sex stories and images and composing brief notes to accompany them would hardly fit a strict, traditional definition of art making. But in an age that accepts the appropriation and curating of images (often sexual ones) as part of the work of an artist, an overly restrictive definition of art would no longer seem to have much use.

Boyd did not join the social circles that came to be known as the New York art world. He knew if he cultivated the impression that we was an artist, he would risk alienating his core audience with a claim that he himself would have been inclined to dismiss as pretentious. And yet figures in the art world were among the first to recognize the value of what he was doing. In issue 17 (1975) of *Straight to Hell*, Boyd printed a fan letter from an unidentified artist:

NEW YORK CITY. I like your magazine very much. I am editing a special issue of a very good art magazine, *Art-Rite*, which I would like to ask you to contribute to if you have anything to say to or about the art world. I am an artist and a very good friend of the editors of this magazine, which is not a gay magazine but is definitely an advanced one. The special issue is on gayness and art, which includes everything from art history scandals to new pornographic art forms. If you're interested in *Art-Rite* it's at 176 Lafayette Street, Apartment #6, New York City 10013. It costs about 50¢ a copy. I think your sports, fashion, and political analyses are terrific.

Art-Rite was published 1973–1978 and edited by Walter Robinson, Edit DeAk, and Joshua Cohn. Cheaply produced on newsprint, it resembled a fanzine or an artist's project and was available for free in commercial art galleries. The artist who sent the letter to Boyd was probably Scott Burton (1939–1989). His papers in the Museum of Modern Art Archives include files of gay cultural materials, including "1960s–1970s gay-themed newsletters and typescript pornography catalogues." MoMA's index of the papers states that these files "seem to relate to Burton's editorship of *Art-Rite* magazine and his involvement with gay culture in and outside the arts, but little evidence is present of Burton's actual activities and functions in this area."

In 1977, Boyd discovered that photographer Robert Mapplethorpe was among *Straight to Hell*'s subscribers. Boyd sent him a questionnaire and published the responses in issue 38:

> *How many times a day do you jack off?* I don't jack off so often anymore as I don't have too much need to; I have an enormous amount of the real thing.
>
> *How often do you like to have sex?* Every day.
>
> *How many people have you had it with?* I couldn't begin to estimate.
>
> *What is your dick like?* I have a dick that I'm comfortable with. I think it better to leave something to mystery.
>
> *Are you circumcised?* Yes.
>
> *Do you care?* I have no choice so I don't care.

Are you glad you have a cock?   Of course. It's my most loved, most prized possession.

Do you have a nice ass?   Very small and very nice.

Is your dick and asshole hair as nice as your armpit hair, shown in Issue 36?   Better.

Do your underpants smell good?   I prefer a jock strap. Of course it smells good.

How does your body look to you in the mirror?   It looks pretty good in all positions—standing, sitting, lying down.

Do my questions exaggerate your interest in getting laid?   No, they don't exaggerate anything. I'm sexually obsessed.

Do you enjoy a life of debauchery?   I suppose I qualify as a sex pervert. I like a bit of kink. The leather bars are my usual hangouts, specifically the Mineshaft, which to my way of thinking is the best bar to ever exist anywhere. I've had sex in all kinds of environments but in the end I prefer private sex in my own loft.

Who are some of the celebrities you've photographed?   Though I have photographed what are known as "celebrities," I don't really think of them in those terms. I don't photograph people I don't like, and most of them are my friends. I suppose Arnold Schwarzenegger would be one as well as Princess Margaret, Patti Smith, Dennis Hopper, David Hockney, etc. They've all got problems just like the rest of us.

How did you happen to become, among other things, a photographer for Warhol?   I had seen Andy around for a number of years. At a certain point I was photographing the same people he was using in his magazine. It just seemed to make sense publishing them in *Interview*.

Do you plan to publish a collection of your photographs in book form? Someday I will publish a book but only when I think there is a chance of its being a best seller.

Where have you lived? I was born on Long Island and moved to Manhattan seven or eight years ago. I get away as often as possible but NYC is my home.

Do you live in a dangerous neighborhood? Some people would say so.

How do you handle it? I try not to think of such things. Some people attract danger. Fortunately, I don't seem to be one of them.

Do you live alone or with someone? Alone.

Why? Because I like it that way. Freedom is very important to me.

Who are some of your heroes? I've never had any real heroes. I think they tend to be disappointing in the flesh. I rather enjoy being myself.

What do you think of the political parties and their recent Presidents? I've never voted in an election.

Do you think America has been on the skids lately? All I know is that my life has gotten better.

Are there any downtrodden people that you feel a special compassion for? No. I'm too egocentric to even consider any of that.

Apart from the celebrities you've photographed, who are some of the other celebrities you know? As I said before, I'm not into celebrities, just people.

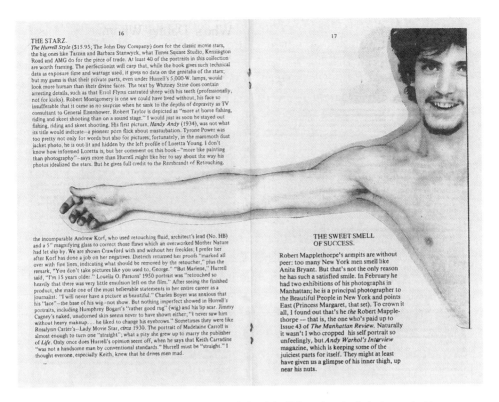

Robert Mapplethorpe assured Boyd that his dick and asshole hair was better than his armpit hair.

How does New York treat you? Any hassles? Life is filled with hassles. I've just had to learn how to take care of myself.

What's a typical day's schedule? I go from downtown to uptown to midtown to downtown. Lunch with the Beautiful People and after dinner I go to the Mineshaft.

Do you admire the Beautiful People? The beautiful, the rich—there are fantastic people in all categories. They add something to my life.

What kind of social life do you have? I have a rather hectic social life, but I wouldn't except that I do enjoy it.

Do you read a daily newspaper? I try to take a look at the papers daily—though lately I haven't really had much of a chance to even do that.

Do you watch TV? No. I had my fill of television as a child.

Do you go to the movies? I prefer real life to movies. The last movie I really enjoyed was *Mandingo*.

Do you read many books? I read books very rarely as I just can't make time. Magazines and newspapers are about the extent of my literary interests at the moment.

Do you consume culture at Lincoln Center? I occasionally go to the ballet if I'm handed tickets, but I prefer sex to all other kinds of culture.

As a young boy, were you made to feel inadequate in any way by other boys and girls? Of course I had problems like everyone. I couldn't care less about such things today. I've learned to be happy with the way I am.

What kind of boyhood sex did you have? I played doctor and all that. I've been experimenting ever since. I rather think in terms of the future.

How does the future look? Dangerous but bright. I'm looking forward to the future.

What by-line do you use on your photographs, just Mapplethorpe or Robert Mapplethorpe? Robert Mapplethorpe.

Boyd considered Mapplethorpe one of "his men"—completely unapologetic, more interested in sex than the ballet, a tough New Yorker who makes a show of being tough, ambitious and egotistical but not hypocritical about it. Boyd returns to his perpetual topics: childhood sex experiences and feelings of inadequacy, underwear and how it smells, celebrities, politics, masturbation. Mapplethorpe, aware that he is on the verge of becoming very famous, hedges a little—for instance, he does not describe his penis or recount specific sex stories—but he is straightforward and succinct in the answers he does provide. Perhaps he realized even then that his words divulged to an underground figure would one day be reproduced in a book.

Robert Mapplethorpe was drawn to the unique qualities of Boyd's work, as a number of older literary figures had been. These writers and artists were in the advance guard of a wave of wider acceptance for *Straight to Hell*. Nowadays younger people who love *STH* take it for granted that Boyd's self-effacing, superficially amateurish, and thoroughly disreputable project is important art.

ON THE QUESTION of Boyd McDonald as an artist, the US court system—which, it must be noted, has generally been *retardataire* when it comes to debates about art—registers complete disagreement with the fans of *Straight to Hell*'s aesthetic. An official view of Boyd's work can be found in *Farrell v. Burke*, decided in 2006 by the United States Court of Appeals, Second Circuit. The opinion was written by Sonia Sotomayor three years before she became Justice of the United States Supreme Court.

Christopher Farrell was convicted in the state of New York of sodomy in the third degree (for paying boys ages 13 to 16 to have sex with him), and after serving almost four years in prison, he was released on parole. A special condition of his parole prohibited the possession of pornographic material. After a parole officer found copies of the summer 1989 issue of the zine *My Comrade* headlined "Gay Sex! The Shocking Truth!," the anthology *Best Gay Erotica 1996*, and *Scum: True Homosexual Experiences* (1993) edited by

Boyd McDonald in Farrell's apartment, he was sent back to prison. Farrell filed an appeal in federal court to challenge the revocation of his parole; at issue was the definition of pornography.

Of the three publications, Boyd McDonald's *Scum* was the main focus of the case. *My Comrade* and *Best Gay Erotica*, according to Sotomayor, "are less obviously prurient in nature. *My Comrade* is satirical; although it deals with sex, it appears intended more to amuse than to arouse.... *Best Gay Erotica 1996* is not in the record in this case. At some point after the arrest, [parole officer] Burke decided that, because the book did not contain any pictures, it was not pornography." Sotomayor discusses Boyd's book in considerable detail:

> *Scum* contains about 25 pictures of men. In all but three of the pictures, the men are nude. In about half of the pictures, the men's penises are erect, and some of the men appear to be touching themselves. A disclaimer on page four of *Scum* states that "[a]ll models are over 18." The State has not challenged this disclaimer.

> The text of *Scum* consists almost entirely of erotic stories describing sexual encounters in intimate detail. Because this case turns on whether the contents of *Scum* are so inarguably "pornographic" as to fit within any reasonable definition of that term, it is necessary to describe with some thoroughness what the book depicts and how it is depicted. The text on the back cover of *Scum* gives a fair picture of its contents:

> > *Scum* is the thirteenth in Boyd McDonald's best-selling series of *Straight to Hell* chapbooks. Like earlier titles... *Scum* contains dozens and dozens of true homosexual experiences. Men from all over write the naked, shameless truth in stories like, "Youth Displays Shit-Hole for Dog to Sniff, Lick," "Soldiers Grope Each Other in Back Row of Theater," "Pushes

Cover design for the thirteenth and last *Straight to Hell* anthology. "The stories that compose *Scum* contain virtually no descriptions of anything other than sex."

Partner's Face into Puddle of Piss," "Army Officer Sniffs Soldier's Jockey Shorts," "Suck Stops on the Highways of Vermont," "US Marine Displays Dick, Butt to Cubans," "Wipes Asshole with His Tongue, Then Screws It with His Tool," and "Cleric Fucks Army Vet's Mouth." Plus there's Boyd McDonald's incomparable "Sex in the News," and plenty of sexy photos, making *Scum* one of the hottest reads ever!

The stories that compose *Scum* contain virtually no descriptions of anything other than sex. The "Sex in the News" sections referenced on the back cover include "news" stories such as "Man Sucks Dick in Front of Café" and "Man, 27, Prowls Naked in Ashtabula."

A number of the stories in *Scum* explicitly describe sex between men and boys. One involves a male "in his late teens" and another male who "looked to be about 60" having sex with multiple other men in a theater bathroom. Another story involves a boy of 14 "being taken into and kicked out of homes of various sugar daddies." A third story notes a news story about a 13-year-old boy who impregnated his 17-year-old baby sitter. The author suggests that he would like to pay the 13-year-old for sex:

> If I was the baby sitter for a 13-year-old boy who wanted to get his rocks off, I could provide him with the same sort of pleasure—or better—and the consequences would be that he would not have to pay child support, he might be a little richer himself, and a child would not be produced.

Elsewhere, a narrator remembers, "[w]hen [I was] nine or ten, my first major mystery occurred. Upon rounding a corner, I found

Red spitting on his 'thing.' So my neighbor Red explained the mystery, instructing me how to pump myself up and down." Other narrators appear to take particular pride in recounting the significantly lower ages of their partners. "I was 49 yrs., he 20½ and a great bed partner." "I was 52 and he only 26." Another narrator regrets that one partner has fully grown up ("He is 25 now and has lost his earlier cuteness") before turning to describe another partner who "first started having sex—and liking it—with his stepfather when he was nine years old and has been turning tricks since his teens."

Numerous stories in *Scum* describe sex between boys. In the first story in the book, for example ("He Liked to Fuck My Face for Half an Hour"), the narrator remembers a series of sexual experiences that occurred "when [he] was a teenager.... Sometimes we would drive around the hills and he would pretend like he was kidnapping me, tie up my body, and then fuck my face." In another story, the author says he had "sucked around from age six or seven, sucking all my elementary school male class mates, then on into high school." Representative stories involving underage boys include a story called "Milwaukee Prodigy, 16, Takes on Two at a Time," and a story about two boys at summer camp having sex called "His Dick Was Sticking Out of His Pajamas." *Scum* graphically describes boys in their early teens having sexual encounters in pools, in locker rooms, in the woods, in garages, and in France, where one narrator remembers "when [he] was 16" and his partner "was 11½." *Scum* contains other examples of stories involving young boys; rather than recount them here, we merely note that the examples cited thus far are all taken from the first half of the book.

Thus *Straight to Hell* entered the public record of the United States Government. When the above description was written, Boyd had been dead for 13 years.

Christopher Farrell did not specifically defend Boyd as an artist, but he did testify that the publication he possessed should not be prohibited because of its redeeming social and historical value.

> Farrell claimed to believe that the word "pornography" included only materials designed solely to arouse sexual appetite. He stated that he believed pornography was "[t]he kind of stuff that you would get in an adult book store or an x-rated movie or a book that has pictures of people engaging in sex activity where the whole purpose of the book is to arouse your sexual appetite." Asked, "What would you think of as a pornographic book?" Farrell responded: "A book that has pictures of people engaging in sexual activity, a video tape of a similar nature and a book whose sole purpose is to pander with people's sexual arousal." Farrell conceded that there were "pictures of men with erections in [*Scum*]," but denied that this made the book pornographic, characterizing it as "not... exaggerated or one-minded depictions of sexual life... [It] makes an attempt to get real gender material so you can have history of the way homosexuals lead their lives."

> We do not agree with Farrell's characterization of *Scum* as "real gender material." Aside from a few paragraphs at the beginning and end of the book, *Scum* makes little pretense of being a work of sexual ethnography. Pictures of nude, aroused men may not always render something "pornographic"—... reasonable people disagree about the nature of Robert Mapplethorpe's pictures— but the pictures in *Scum* appear alongside stories that are as wholly designed "to arouse your sexual appetite" as any we can imagine. *Scum* thus fits precisely within Farrell's definition of "pornography" as "a book that has pictures of people engaging

in sex activity where the whole purpose of the book is to arouse your sexual appetite."

The panel of judges rejected Christopher Farrell's appeal. Sotomayor's opinion contains a slight inaccuracy: it mentions "pictures of people engaging in sex activity," but there are none in *Scum*. Pictures of nude men, sometimes in a state of arousal, appear in all of Boyd's publications, but sexual activity is described only in the texts of *Straight to Hell* anthologies.

Sonia Sotomayor admitted the difficulties of ruling that any material is pornographic:

> For purposes of evaluating artistic or cultural merit, the term "pornography" is notoriously elusive. In that context, determining whether material deserves the label of pornography is a subjective, standardless process, heavily influenced by the individual, social and cultural experience of the person making the determination…. Whether or not the term "pornography" is inherently vague, *Scum* fits within any reasonable understanding of the term.

It is a posthumous tribute to Boyd that his work inspired long and thorough reflection by one of the most powerful people in the world.

IN A DISCLAIMER found in the colophon of *Wads*, Boyd stated his position on an issue related to *Farrell v. Burke*: "It is against the law to have intercourse with boys under 18, but we do print memoirs of men talking about their own boyhood experiences." Responding to concerns about having no "proof of age on file" for models in the photographs illustrating his books—to comply with the 2257 regulations that US federal law enforcement has used since the 1990s as a means ostensibly to protect children, but covertly to hound the porn industry out of existence—Boyd wrote to his publisher, Harold

Norse, "I've decided to solve the problem of underage youth by simply not giving their ages. That's legal." Amid the shifting boundaries between art and pornography and waves of child abuse hysteria, this attitude seems reckless today, but Boyd did his work in different times.

Due to changes in legal standards since the early 1970s, a portion of the material that appeared in early issues of *Straight to Hell* is untouchable by mainstream publishers. As Billy Miller says, a reprint of the original chapbooks would be

> currently impossible without doing a whole lot of cutting and editing. In Boyd's day and in the beginning when I started publishing the series, there were still lots of dirty bookstores— which were, along with gay bookstores like A Different Light, Giovanni's Room, and others, the primary outlet for the chapbooks and the magazines that featured Boyd's writing. All that is over now and everything is online. It's a completely different market.

Boyd's own collection of pictures and magazines, whatever it may have contained, got him into trouble in the place where he once lived, the Empire Hotel. He told Jim Tamulis in a letter,

> I had maid service at the Empire and I guess the maid or housekeeper ratted to the mgt. and they inspected my room. It's not quite as simple as being evicted on a porn rap—I was storing back issues of *STH* there and they could have got me on a fire hazard rap. But the mgr. did say I was storing porn in my room. I didn't fight it—it's silly in this culture to bring work like mine to the attention of rednecks. They could easily put me in jail if they wanted to, or rather if they knew about it. I was given two weeks' notice and found a bigger room, same price, and am happy as can be. People like me get their happiness from work not real estate.

Boyd in 1981. "They didn't even have the word 'sex-addict' then or anything, but it looked like he had just jerked off on that cot."

The place to which Boyd moved—room 6-N-6, Riverside Studios, 342 West 71st Street, New York—was where he would spend the rest of his life.

AFTER THE PUBLICATION of the first *Straight to Hell* anthology, *Meat* (1981), Boyd emerged to become something like a public figure. The *Village Voice* had mentioned *Straight to Hell* as early as 1974, but at that point, its editor preferred to remain anonymous. A 1981 *Voice* article by Vince Aletti features a photograph of Boyd on his bed, and it caught the attention of some readers. John Waters shares his thoughts about it: "He lived in a single rented room and slept on a cot. That awesome picture, which he of course released himself, was great, so shocking because it was off the grid…. They didn't even have the word 'sex-addict' then or anything, but it looked like he had just jerked off on that cot." In his profile of Boyd, Vince describes the details of this rented room on the Upper West Side, and its occupant, who seemed elderly and frail, even though he was only 55 years old at the time. Vince's initial impression was that Boyd looked like a derelict, yet there was something prim and proper about him. He thought Boyd resembled William S. Burroughs. In my conversation with Vince, I ventured that McDonald and Burroughs were both examples of a type I call the "Ivy League fuck-up." Vince laughed and said, "Boyd would have been pleased by that."

When I asked Vince how he discovered *Straight to Hell*, he told me that he had found it at Gay Treasures in the West Village. According to the masthead of issues from the mid-1970s, *STH* was sold only in five bookstores at first. It was not on sale at Greenwich Village's oldest gay bookstore, the Oscar Wilde Bookshop. Craig Rodwell, the owner, disapproved of it and told customers that all of its stories had been made up by Boyd himself. Any issue of *Straight to Hell* contains such a wide variety of voices and experiences that this rumor can only be believed by those who have never actually read *STH*, who think that all sexually explicit writing is more or less the same, or who deny that those sexual experiences had ever really happened and indeed are still happening all around them. Stephen Greco, whose *Advocate* interview with Boyd came out a few months after the *Voice* article, originally had his doubts:

> The big question on my mind was, "Are all these letters real?" I thought anybody literary could come up with different voices. It was like a vaudeville routine. He went to a closet, opened the door, and literally out of it fell Santa Claus bags full of correspondence. He let me look through it. Every sort of handwriting. Every sort of envelope. It was all real.

Boyd explained to any interviewer who asked that he edited the texts he received from correspondents, sometimes heavily, but never paraphrased or invented.

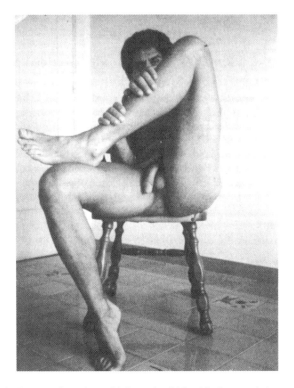

Rimmer's digest: a *Straight to Hell* reader hides his face and shows his ass.

BOYD WAS CONVINCED that the truth of male sexuality bore little resemblance to received wisdom about it, and on this point he followed Alfred Kinsey. A biologist whose original field was entomology, Kinsey founded the Institute for Sex Research at Indiana University in 1947. The next year, he published the book *Sexual Behavior in the Human Male*, which contained a provocative finding: nearly half of the adult male population in the US had had at least one homosexual experience. This provoked much denial at first, but it triggered a drastic shift in attitudes toward homosexuality. Kinsey based his conclusions on a vast number of interviews he and his staff of researchers conducted with American men from all strata of society. Boyd self-consciously imitated aspects of Kinsey's methodology but used the medium of written texts rather than in-person interviews. Instead of statistics, Boyd presented personal narratives, or as he put it, "true case histories in the tradition of Kinsey."

One part of Alfred Kinsey's work which Boyd did not use was the Kinsey scale introduced in *Sexual Behavior in the Human Male*. It classified "socio-sexual contacts or reactions" along a scale of 0 (exclusively heterosexual) to 6 (exclusively homosexual). While it has been criticized for being too crude a measurement, the idea of the scale has proven fundamental and has been widely used with refinements and variations ever since. In *Sexual Behavior in the Human Male*, Kinsey sums up his position:

> Males do not represent two discrete populations, heterosexual and homosexual. The world is not to be divided into sheep and goats. It is a fundamental of taxonomy that nature rarely deals with discrete categories.... The living world is a continuum in each and every one of its aspects.

Boyd was reluctant to use the word "bisexual"—generally absent from legal definitions and political discourse to this day—but he did recognize (though not explicitly) the poverty of labels and the wide variation of human desires, especially when it worked to the advantage of a horny man in search of available male flesh.

In the midst of disorganized stacks of letters, Boyd compiled his data like a social science researcher, but he approached his task without any attempt at objectivity. The *Straight to Hell* contributors whose sex stories interested him but were lacking in specifics would receive questionnaires requesting descriptions of sights, smells, and tastes in extreme detail. But even Boyd had his limits. In the *Village Voice* interview, he told Vince Aletti, "I have a terrific article from a guy who likes to eat cops' shit. On that subject it's the definitive piece, but that's so specialized." Boyd also had little interest in stories involving sex toys or fisting, though a couple of drawings of fist fucking appear in early issues of *STH*; spontaneity and genital contact (however brief) were his priorities. Exactly what preferences compelled Boyd to choose the stories he did remain somewhat obscure—just as Alfred

ESPIONAGE   Ex-C.I.A. Operative Asks
            To See Our Mailing Lists

A former operative of the U.S. Government's Counter Intelligence Agency has
written asking if he may look at our mailing lists.
    But there is no cause for alarm. The ex-spy has reformed and is looking for
cocks to suck in the New York Metropolitan Region, not homosexuals to black-
mail. He describes himself as uncut, married, a father, and an expert cocksucker who likes to have men suck him off as well.
    "If I get to N.Y.C.," he wrote, "would you be agreeable to my scanning the
address files? I could recognize the names of the small towns much better than
a stranger. Besides my former C.I.A. training is very handy for that sort of
thing. Hell, yes, I used to believe the crap the Establishment fed me before
I learned to think clearly. That was some time ago."
    We replied that our files are Top Secret but that we find some faint hope
for America if even one C.I.A. spook has stopped sneaking around spying on
other people and has come clean and gone straight, with such positive hobbies
as cocksucking.

LETTERS   Subscriber Wants
            To Smell Asshole

Pennsylvania. I will admit I really
enjoy the smells and tastes of the
whole male body, so why not give me
a break? I sure would love to be your
obedient slave and sure would love to
smell your asshole and everything that
goes with it. What do you say? Will
you please give me a break and let me
smell your pants and have a taste?

THE MILITARY   Air Force Guy Takes
               37 Cocks Up Asshole
               In One Session

A.P.O. San Francisco. Enclosed is my
story which actually occurred. I'm
not sure if you'd print it but it sure
as hell happened.
    Heard about this construction site
with a lot of horny studs. I'm 24,
6' 1" tall, 165 lbs., white & love to
get fucked...gang fucked. Wore cut-
offs and hung around the front gate
at closing time. A dude eyed me and
gave me the once over and invited me
in. He was in his late 20s and was
pretty rugged looking. Lead me to a
trailer and ripped my Levis off. My
head was immediately kissing a desk
top and my bare ass protruding over
the desk. Talk about getting fucked
rough! Heard the door open and more
dudes walked in grabbing for their
zippers. A big black dude with a
thick 10½ incher rammed me for 20
fucking minutes till the other guys
told him to get out. I then proceed-
ed to take on 37 dudes for the next
seven hours. To get guys up for it
quicker I started a line in front as
well as in back and sucked off dudes.
Got cream in my mouth and in my ass.
My asshole was raw but well-fucked
and I'd like to go back for more.

STRAIGHT TO HELL

THE AMERICAN
JOURNAL OF
REVENGE
THERAPY

Box 982
Radio
City
Station
NYC 10019

50¢ a copy

12 issues,
4 bucks

Checks
Payable
To Cash

#6
1974

The American Journal of Revenge Therapy—Straight to Hell issue 6 (1974).

Kinsey's homosexual experiences were kept secret during his lifetime. Both men projected a combination of remoteness and approachability that enabled them to elicit the most private details of the sex lives of total strangers.

During the early years of *Straight to Hell*, men wrote to Boyd spontaneously; perhaps a fair number of them were surprised to read that others felt and acted the same way they did and were moved to add their stories to Boyd's collections. By the early 1980s, because knowledge of Boyd's work and of homosexuality in general began to influence the sample population, fewer men wrote to him without encouragement, and the function of the questionnaires changed. He told Winston Leyland of Gay Sunshine Press, the publisher of *Meat*,

> I am receiving astonishing material daily, both at my home address (which I give to regular *STH* writers) and the P. O. address (which I use for men I don't know well). More than usual of it is questionnaires; the voluntary narratives aren't coming in at all, and every letter I get for publication I have to ask for, with detailed instructions that I don't want porn but anti-porn.

The wide commercial availability of pornography in the US had accustomed many men to the generic conventions of fictional sex writing, and had made Boyd's search for truth much more complex and difficult.

Boyd developed extended epistolary relationships over the course of editing *Straight to Hell* and the paperback anthologies. Some of his correspondents wrote entire sexual autobiographies over numerous installments and had hopes of publishing their own books. Boyd recommended their work to Gay Sunshine Press. Of special note are two highly literate Classicists—in letters to Leyland, Boyd calls them "Englishman #1" and "Englishman #2," though the former was Scottish—and an American named Jim Dugan, whose tales of his Uncle Joe (born 1888), published in five installments in *Straight to Hell* issues 23–27, are among the earliest testimonies Boyd ever received. Whether Boyd revealed to any of these men the details of his own sex life is unknown. On the subject of Boyd's sexual experiences, Vince Aletti expressed regret that he didn't ask and Boyd didn't offer anything. His demeanor was so studious and upright that the topic didn't even come up in conversation. Boyd had a silent way of deflecting attention away from his own life.

OF ALL THE FRIENDS of Boyd McDonald I have been able to interview, Billy Miller has the clearest recollection of his personal life:

> I am sure he was sexually active before I met him, and he did mention some guy who had been over there during the time I was hanging out there a lot, but he was in general a sort of ascetic and lived with practically nothing.
>
> During the years of our friendship, I never knew him to buy much of anything. It was so hot one summer that I got a fan for him. He said he didn't need it, although he was sweating and with the non-circulating cigarette smoke (because the window opened onto an air shaft with no real breeze) it was stifling in there, to say the least. But then the week after, he admitted that the fan was a good idea and added that he was amazed that it actually made a difference…. He liked to have nothing, and any sort of luxury at all was some sort of sin that caused him a lot of mental strife.
>
> He was very smart and clever, but also what just about anyone would call crazy. He talked to several people on the phone, some of them people like Gore Vidal. And fans would make pilgrimages to his monk cell in the SRO, but at that point (the 1980s) he didn't go anywhere, or see anyone, unless they came to him. His days were focused on his writing and on personal battles with demons real and imagined. Towards the end of his life he was so nutty and curmudgeonly that I stopped seeing him so often; it was also more than I could deal with, as I had my own problems.

For about five years we were close friends and talked weekly, and I saw him often. Around 1988 or 89, he all of a sudden told me I should start editing and publishing *STH*, since Victor Weaver [the editor since 1981] was moving to England and had lost interest in the project. (Boyd had several years earlier stopped publishing the original chapbook series in favor of his magazine writing and book projects.) Then he gave me several bags full of contributors' letters and called Victor up and arranged for me to get the keys to the storage place where all the back issues and index cards with the subscribers' addresses, etc., were stored.

We never talked about *STH*, actually, but mostly talked about books that he or I were reading, or about things in the news. He talked about doing a publication called "Sex in the News," along with other ideas he was always coming up with. He loved to use topical things in the news as a springboard for his commentaries and liked to come up with funny headlines inspired by tabloid-speak. And he also loved to take the piss out of fancy pretentious people and things. He saw that I was as full of hate for that shit as he was, so that was enough to be the basis of a friendship. I think he also had a sort of crush on me initially, but after a while it was more about cracking each other up.

The guy at the desk downstairs would announce you before you went up to whatever room by calling first. So one time when I got off the elevator and went past those other dingy rooms, I saw that the door to his room was slightly ajar and that the lights were off and his room was dark, which I thought odd. Then when I got to the door, I knocked, pushed it open slightly and said, "Boyd?" but didn't see anyone at first. Then I saw the pinpoint flare of a cigarette being puffed on and realized he was there. When I opened the door wider, more of the light from the hallway went into the room, and I saw him sitting there with a knit ski mask on, smoking a cigarette through the mask. That was his droll sense of humor.

He was full of vitriol about so many things, but so polite and proper in every way. He was never petty or unkind and was again, almost martyr-like. He would literally give you his last dollar, which he did for me at least a couple times.

Billy wasn't the only friend Boyd helped. During the video interview conducted in 1989, there is an interruption; someone who had borrowed money from Boyd came over to pay him back. He explained that he regularly lent money at no interest to a number of his fellow SRO residents.

Elaborating on what he shared with Boyd, Billy adds, "I've always gotten along well with people of his age group, because I'm a jazz and old movie fan—which are two of the things we talked about a lot."

IN 1983, Boyd began writing a column about old movies for the gay literary magazine *Christopher Street*. After an initial telephone call introducing himself, he wrote a letter to Tom Steele, the editor. In it he summarizes his sexual and political obsessions succinctly, and tells how they are related.

Dear Tom Steele:

You mentioned over the 'phone that you're using my "Great Moments in Movies".... Also that I should contact you about writing more for the magazine.

My work is of two main types: questionnaires with men about their sexual experiences and my reviews of the news, sports, pictures, TV, books and so on....

I do these questionnaires for my books (three in print, two being set in type, three in progress). I also write reviews for these books, such as:

(1) "Cocksucking and Catholicism." Catholics who've seen this think it's hilarious. Winston Leyland, a former priest, is using it in his next anthology of my work. It's not as radical as it sounds—for years the Catholic Church has been a target of the conservative Gay Establishment, as can be seen in the annual gay parades past St. Patrick's.

(2) "Great Moments in TV." Enthusiastic but funny fan notes about Ricky Nelson and Steven Ford. Steven was at Uncle Charley's [a Midtown Manhattan gay bar], according to Liz Smith, and now is on a soap opera. He's the former President's son and painfully handsome. The Great Moment is when the other actor in the frame bends down to pick something up and Steven lowers his eyes to look at the actor's ass....

(3) "Sex Acts," using "Acts" as a pun, since most of the men in this collection of items are actors: Tony Perkins, William Atherton, Eddie Murphy, Jimmy Connors (tennis). It's a negative article about their pretense and not too long. Perkins and Atherton are "former homosexuals." Former homosexuals are like former Irishmen. Perkins appeared in an anti-porn parade in Times Square at a time when his own ass was under fire from both straight and gay critics not for being bare in a rotten Broadway play but for being too puny. In contrast to the fully developed butts displayed in the Times Square street. This is almost always *de rigueur* for prudery. The prude is beneath sex, not, as he claims, above it. Atherton's face in *Day of the Locust* with his huge, pretty mouth wide open in horror would make a best selling poster, but as an Aesthetic Realist he naturally wouldn't permit it. Perkins's homosexuality is official (*People* magazine). Eddie Murphy jokes

24

Simpson

O.J. IN A JOCK STRAP.

STANFORD, CALIFORNIA.—Before coming to Stanford, I was working in Hollywood and going to U.S.C. part time. This must have been during O.J. Simpson's last year at U.S.C. (1969-1970). Because I used to run, lift weights, swim and generally hang out at the gym, I met O.J. a number of times. One afternoon I was in the weight room working on an exercise machine called Universal Gym. The leg press part is lowest to the floor and faces the South wall, which is covered with mirrors (for narcissism). I was on this part of the machine when O.J. and a couple of his Black buddies came in to work out. They were bareassed except for bulging jock straps. We exchanged nods and greetings and O.J. came over to work on the bench press section which was raised and to my left. Since I'd seen O.J. stripped to gym shorts several times before, I already knew he had a great Bod: thick neck and arms, gigantic thighs, and beautiful dark reddish brown skin. So this time I concentrated on the private parts. His jock pouch was filled out quite well and because the bench press user has to spread his legs wide to the sides of the bench, he gave me a fantastic panoramic view of his beautiful tight buns bulging out of the jock; dark, moist curly-haired crack; fuzzy crotch; plus just a hint of asshole and a teasing peek of one large thick wrinkled nut sac. All in a juicy mouth-watering stud. I wonder if the sports writers realize how appropriate his pro nick-name, "The Juice," really is. P.S. Yes, it's true about jock straps lying around college locker rooms.

O. J. Simpson flops around the gym: *Straight to Hell* issue 32 (1977).

about AIDS and speaks of "faggot-assed faggots".… The item would give the standard psychological explanation, which even Ann Landers now uses, for Murphy's obsessive fag-baiting. For Connors I'd cite his homosexual horseplay from a recent book and, unlike the author, relate it to another item in the book: that Connors is never seen without a towel in the locker rooms. On the courts he motions for the referees to suck his dick, but perhaps he doesn't have a big enough one to make such an act rewarding.…

(4) "Typical Heterosexuals." A series of news photographs of the grossest heterosexuals with captions which stick strictly to the

facts but are written in heavy irony ("Alone and unarmed, he heroically subdued a three-year-old girl, made love to her mouth with his penis and held her head under muddy water until she stopped struggling.") Another example is a photo of Reagan's former EPA head, Anne Burford, struggling to get her big fat ass into a car; it's not the size of her ass that distresses me so much as its cleanliness and that of her boss, President Reagan, if they are as careless with personal daintiness as they are with polluting the environment. Pro sports stars with limp wrists. An endless supply of negative photos of heterosexuals.

(5) "The Straight Life." A collection of news items, written without comment (the headline being the only comment necessary), about murder, rape, incest, child torture, and so forth. An endless supply. Also photos of known or suspected homosexuals with women: Tommy Tune with Twiggy, Halston with Liza Minnelli, Warhol, the President's son with his wife, and so on.

(6) "The Gay Life." A series, like "The Straight Life," which could run periodically as a collection of news items. Under this head I'd put heterosexual homosexuals: football coach arrested for sucking dick, etc. Fraternity "straight queers."

(7) "Sports Builds Character." A collection of news items which could run periodically: corruption, murder, rape, drugs, gambling, assorted sports scandals. I think this would be popular with homosexual readers who are bullied for not being good athletes.

(8) "Learn from Your Superiors." A series which would open with a contemptuous quote about homosexuals and then examine the superiority of heterosexuality. E. g., Senator [Henry Martin] Jackson's quote about homosexuals, then an item about his own state (Washington): soldiers were let in by attendants to

"Eating stuff" Pete Rose, switch hitter for the Cincinnati Reds (1963–78), nicknamed "Charlie Hustle," grabs his meat for the camera. The photographer, a *Straight to Hell* subscriber, preferred to remain "anonymous, if you don't mind," so as not to lose access to players on the field and in the locker room.

rape Frances Farmer, the movie actress, in a mental hospital. A Government quote about homosexuals as "security risks," followed by some of the "straight" security risks: Nixon, etc.

(9) "Family Life." Quotes from "family" people like Nancy Reagan, Cardinal [Terence] Cooke, David Denby (the movie reviewer), Anita Bryant, Jerry Falwell, etc. This could be a periodical series: each one opens with a quote, followed by news reports of family life: murder, child abuse, etc. Nancy's could be about the family life of her own friends. E. g. the Bloomingdales, Betsey arrested on smuggling rap. Alfred has S/M mistress. One of the Reagan lawyers [Roy Miller] has a son who is literally a motherfucker: he raped then killed his mother.

(10) Hatchet job on Norman Mailer. Even the Jews have rednecks. Has twice advocated killing as beneficial to the killer. Hatred of women, homosexuals, love of boxers and prison pen pals. But Jack Abbott, his prison pen pal, turned out to be a disappointment: turned up in New York as a slight dandy with a huge pocket handkerchief like a Wall Street waitress, not the Stud who'd written from prison about "us men" who need "women" (homosexuals)—publication of which letter gave Abbott, Mailer and Robert Silvers of *The New York Review of Books* much-needed intimations of virility. Mailer's now out of the closet, after long suspicions, as an authentic and advanced Pervut with specialties in scatology and violent heterosexual homosexuality (buggery). It has never been unusual in literary salons to hear his work referred to as "shitty," but the word has until now been used as a metaphor. With *Ancient Evenings* the adjective has become literally descriptive; two conservative reviewers have called the book "full of shit." It's also full of asshole rape. Mailer announced at Carnegie Hall that he has a "small prick." Worse, he has the biggest teats of any man in public life. (*Rolling Stone* tit photo.) Is Titty Envy on the part of his wives

the reason behind his numerous divorces? Mailer discovered in middle age that homosexuals can't have babies with each other, but have them, as heterosexuals do, with their wives. It's too late to review *Ancient Evenings* but that book would supply material. It's a course in advanced perversions, with Krafft-Ebbing and de Sade as prerequisite reading.

(11) Hatchet job on William F. Buckley, Jr. Talks of a "cure" for homosexuality…. Catholicism has for him the appeal it has for all who lack sexual gifts: it assures them that the thing they're not good at, sex, is wrong anyway. The really rich don't talk about their servants any more than a typist mentions that lunch was brought to her at the coffee shop by a waitress; *service compris*. But after his—and *The New Yorker's*—prolonged attempt at being snobbish with obsessive talk of his servants in his journals published in that magazine, he sabotaged the whole long article by revealing at the end that his mother eats pizza. Worse, he has dandruff (*People* magazine). "The Biggest Queen in New York" (in manner, not sex life); piss elegant peasant. Soft cocked, hard hearted; broad-hipped, narrow-minded; cold assed, hot tempered.

I think I should send items (2) and (3) and see how they go. If nothing else comes of this, at least I was delighted to hear that Margaret Whiting sat on a piano in a short skirt with no underwear. Only today I heard from someone who used to work at Warner's that Barbara Stanwyck gave fantastically foul-mouthed abuse to George Brent when he blew a line and they had to do another take. I don't think it reflects poorly on any of them; Whiting, Stanwyck and Ricky Nelson can do no wrong.

Best,
Boyd McDonald

Diplomacy

It's not just that Henry Kissinger's a warmonger--after all it's estimated that one out of every two American males is also a warmonger. But only a small minority of them pick their noses in public and <u>that's</u> unforgiveable; I'm sorry.

Nobel laureate and former Secretary of State Henry Kissinger picks his nose.

Printer's instructions for *Flesh* (1982).

Although the specific targets of Boyd's satire changed with the times, these were the themes to which he would return repeatedly. In one form or another, most of the texts he described found their way into the pages of *Christopher Street*, other gay publications such as *New York Native, Connection*, and *Philadelphia Gay News*, or the *Straight to Hell* anthologies.

BOYD EXPANDED his possibilities as a writer by approaching political themes. He mentioned a plan for a publication devoted entirely to news items, *Trans Lux*, which was never realized, though various gay magazines ran his "Sex in the News" items. Boyd's mainstay continued to be editing the sex stories contributed by the readers of *Straight to Hell*. Their stories often took the form of reminiscences of youth and had a nostalgic quality. This nostalgia intensified with each successive *STH* anthology in the series through the 1980s, when during the AIDS crisis, many men became more cautious in their sexual practices and law enforcement authorities closed some of the places where public sex occurred. The stories in *STH* books invariably refer to sexual activity before AIDS. The only references to AIDS are in the safer sex guidelines that later editions included at the back.

A number of the best *Straight to Hell* contributions came from older men who were more or less out of the game and waxed eloquent about their conquests of men who appeared unavailable until they were flat on their backs wailing in ecstasy. The guiding principle of the stories is like a lascivious challenge overheard at a gay bar: "He too can be had." The promise of sexual availability (as opposed to a declaration of sexual orientation) animates much of *Straight to Hell*. The scenarios reflect the sensibility of a distant time, the period before gay liberation's collective struggles were widely publicized in the US and the existence of another way of life began to dawn on the squares.

BOYD'S COLLEGE ROOMMATE John Arning was a family man who could pass as a square, but he may have had more in common with Boyd than he was willing to admit. Bill Arning long suspected that his father had homosexual tendencies and would pick up men for sex on the many trips he took for business. John once bought his wife a subscription to *Playgirl* magazine and passed it off as a joke. As a "snoopy kid" looking around while his parents were out of town, Bill found issues of *Playgirl* hidden at the back of his father's closet. When Bill later came out to his family, his father said that he supported him, but added, "If you could get used to women, it would make your life easier." John Arning could have been paraphrasing an item called "Unnatural Act" in *Juice* (1984): "'Anybody,' says Auberon Waugh, the English writer, 'can cultivate a taste for heterosexuality with a little effort.'" This advice—probably offered to Boyd at Harvard many years before—provoked a question in *Flesh*: "Why do boys 'go with' men and marry women? Duty or desire? Duty to whom? Desire for what—women or display?" Boyd invited his readers to tell their own stories: "There are still some people, such as the United States Government, who regard married men as 'straight'…. I always welcome letters… which describe what goes on behind the façade of Holy Matrimony."

SINCE THE WORDS above were written, same-sex marriage in the United States has acquired official legal status and its own façade. Now queer people in loving pairs can experience the conflicts arising from the attempt to maintain two virtuous states simultaneously: truthfulness and matrimony. In the course of legal battles for marriage equality, gay activists discovered that it was better for all concerned to remain quiet on the subject of sexual intercourse. When Edith Windsor, who married Thea Spyer in Canada in 2007, sued the US Government, which obliged her to pay taxes on the estate of her late wife, her attorneys advised her to refrain from revealing anything about the couple's wild sex life. She took the advice and won her suit in 2013. This was the crucial case leading to the Supreme Court's decision to strike down restrictions on same-sex marriage in 2015.

In his introduction to the first *Straight to Hell* anthology, Charles Shively advocates disclosure, but acknowledges the strategic value of dissembling:

> Throughout *Meat* a poignant theme recurs: "The truth is the biggest turn-on." "This is true." "Every word of this is true..." "As I think back on those days today it all seems unbelievable but it happened."... Having spent our whole lives dissimulating and now finding a forum for speech, we are all aghast at the freedom, the possibility. In a society such as ours where people hide what they call their vices, "It would be dangerous to be frank," says Sade's Bedroom Philosopher; "Hypocrisy and lying are enjoined upon us by society." So if you are a postal inspector, psychiatrist, district attorney, censor, border guard, parent, priest or other authority, relax, you have nothing to worry about, everything we say is fiction, lies.

Certain fictions have proven expedient in the winning of queer political power, and Boyd recognized this trend as it developed.

> My work is an alternative to the gay liberation movement and to the gay press. The gay press has to be sexless because they are public. And in order to be publicly gay they have to be closet homosexuals. My books are all about homosexuality rather than gayness. In other words, gay is what they are in public, and homosexual is what they are in private. It has nothing to do with gay liberation, gay rights, gays in the military, civil rights, fundraising, political candidates, and all that stuff. If you're going to be a lobbyist or lawyer running a fundraising campaign, you cannot be sexual. It is a necessity that the whole gay liberation movement had to give up sex in order to go public as gay.

Boyd did not accept that proper, discreet behavior is, or should be, rewarded with tolerance. "I wouldn't try to please the stupid people. That's what some homosexuals think we should try to do. It won't work because the bigotry

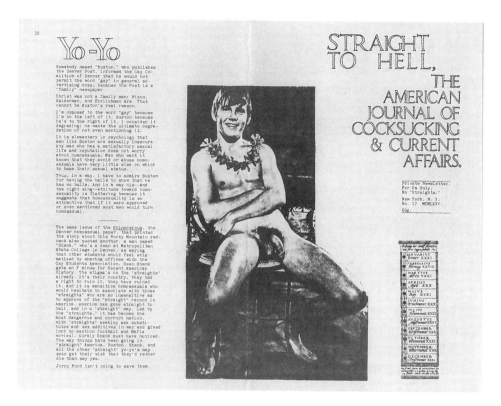

Cocksucking and current affairs—*Straight to Hell* issue 17 (1975).

comes not from the behavior of the minority but from the mind of the bigot." He offered these words in his last interview with *The Guide* in 1993; the ways of assimilation have changed little since then.

IN THE ARTICLE "The Male Homosexual and Marriage," John McAndrews writes, "The invert, it seems to me, should live alone and learn to like it, and to be self-sufficing." The essay was published in 1961 by *Der Kreis* (The Circle). This Swiss journal promoted gay rights by means of an assimilationist program.

The goal of *Der Kreis* is the complete integration of gay men into existing society. Its respect is to be gained through special effort and strict accommodation to prevailing norms…. The coupled relationship, set above all… as the only gay form of life, mirror[s] traditional marriage.

McAndrews disagreed with such rigidly conformist politics, but nonetheless contributed frequently to the journal, and lobbied its editors to expand the range of (very chaste) writing it accepted. "John McAndrews" was in fact the pseudonym of Samuel Steward (1909–1993), an English professor at Catholic universities, a fan of Gertrude Stein and Alice B. Toklas, a pornographer under the name Phil Andros, and a tattoo artist in Chicago and Oakland. He was also an aspiring novelist, but he never realized his potential, because his chief leisure activity and his subject matter were one and the same: having sex with as many men as possible. His stories were not publishable during the prime of his life, and his sexual pursuits consumed so much time and energy that he could not concentrate on becoming the sort of serious man of letters who composed veiled accounts of his true appetites and inclinations. Instead, Steward achieved a distinction that does not bring the public accolades of academic or literary success—he became a brilliantly prodigious sex artist.

BOYD MCDONALD points out that *Cum* (1983) is special in his preface to the volume:

This is the fourth anthology of letters written by readers of the magazine I founded, *STH (Straight to Hell): The New York Review of Cocksucking*.

This book differs from its three predecessors… in that most of the letters in it have never been published before….

In my lovely home, I still have shopping bags full of unpublished letters. New ones arrive daily. I hope to put all of those which seem true into other books pronto; after all, I am inspired by them too.

Another of the book's attractions is that it contains an anonymous contribution from a well-known person. In the section "Sucks Off 750 Boys, Men," the answers to one of Boyd McDonald's typically probing questionnaires (Ohio, Chicago, priests, teaching jobs) indicate that this was the sexual history of Samuel Steward. As is clear from the title, Steward's main sexual activity was fellatio, performed on trade, men who do not play the passive role in sex—except that a man getting a blow job is actually the passive one, but a piece of trade doesn't think that way—and who do not consider themselves to be homosexual. Even in the small town where he grew up, Steward pursued his preferred object with great success.

Did you ever feel any shame or guilt about your desires or practices? If not why not? Never. I figured I was put in that town just to bring pleasure to the guys I admired. Being raised by maiden aunts, and finding out about sex from my lucky discovery of Havelock Ellis's book [*Studies in the Psychology of Sex, Volume II: Sexual Inversion* (1897)], and not making any connection between sex and the Methodist church, I simply never thought I was doing anything shameful. Had absolutely no guilt.

Were you sexually triumphant because you were in a small town, not in a big city? Of course. Nowadays in a city, everyone would want money. Hustlers.

Were any of the boys rough trade, or just plain trade? Most of them were just plain trade....

You mentioned that you went off to college "with the major purpose of bringing pleasure to straight young men." Why straight? Were homosexuals not interesting? I never wanted reciprocation.... I never propositioned a visibly homosexual boy through university. Sometimes they propositioned me. I never enjoyed being trade in those years.... There were not many rejections, but of course some, from uptight or religious or 100% heteros.

You mentioned that you've kept records. How many people have you had sex with? I have had sex with 807 persons for a total of 4,647 times. Several... numbered over 200 times each, though I never had a "love affair" with anyone or lived with him.... Of the 807, I would guess that I blew 750.... One fucked me over 300 times. One I blew about 275 times. Most of the rest were "repeats" for blow jobs. Kinsey looked at my statistics in 1948 when he interviewed me and said, "Well, that's a respectable total. I've seen some that are a lot more and some a lot less. I'd sort of put you in the middle third." I didn't know whether I was flattered or offended.

Steward's account, of which the above is only a brief excerpt, is factual as far as anyone can determine, and on the whole, positive. He does not dwell on his experiences with rough trade—men who not only consider themselves heterosexual, but also beat up and sometimes rob their partners after taking their pleasure. Nor does Steward indulge in much self-reflection. He is not interested in being someone's psychological case study. The tone is one of detachment, a frame of mind he spent 50 years refining before Boyd corresponded with him. Steward also had a lot of practice recounting his experiences in dispassionate detail: he kept a journal and compiled a cross-referenced catalogue called the Stud File containing cards for every sex partner during his lifetime. He contributed his collection to the Institute for Sex Research at Indiana University.

By CONTEMPORARY STANDARDS normalizing romantic love gay and straight, Boyd McDonald, Samuel Steward, and other contributors to *Straight to Hell* would be considered sexual compulsives. Boyd addresses this question in an editor's note in *Filth*:

> There have been several pious articles in both the "straight" and gay press recently about compulsive promiscuity. I suspect the authors of these articles to be jealous. It is usually suggested that people who are obsessed with sex seek "help." But it is not such gifted and well-functioning people who need help, but rather the sexually cold ones. They make a virtue of their fear, their coldness, and their ordinary, conventional attitude. I regard extreme and frequent sexual heat, and the obsessive, compulsive prowling of people who are seeking to relieve it, as admirable—as a gift—and far more enviable than the writing of those who profess to scorn it. In work and in sex... only people who are obsessed and compelled do extraordinary work and live extraordinary lives. They make ordinary people feel bad.

Boyd considered himself to be extraordinary, and he saw the men who shared their sexual experiences with him in the same way.

JOHN WATERS'S ESSAY "Outsider Porn" in his book *Role Models* (2010) describes impulses that conventionally well-adjusted gay men prefer not to discuss: desire for sex with men who are straight, "straight acting," bisexual, or only hungry—anything but openly gay. He interviews Bobby Garcia, the director who fellated hundreds of horny Marines on camera, and David

Hurles, whose Old Reliable movies, photographs, and audio recordings capture the rages and the erections of rough convicts and hustlers who look as though they could kill him at any time. Hurles told John Waters, "Boyd was the kindest person," who "gave me such encouragement."

Boyd also interviewed Hurles, who explains his criteria as a connoisseur of trade in *Meat*:

> *Are the pricks you photograph naughty-but-nice types or are they authentic bastards?* Most are real pricks and rotten bastards. I wish it were otherwise…. Being a prick is just not enough.

> *Where do you find models?* The street, ads, but mostly by referral from others satisfied with their own experience.

> *How do you proposition them?* Money is the key.

> *What percent of your models are 100% homosexual?* About 20%.

> *What percent are 100% straight?* About 50%. My joys. The remainder are mixed. Pieces of trade fall within that 80%. Whores tend to be a problem. There are too into money, always in a hurry, frequently too spent to be any good, and most of them are crooks…. Fortunately, my trade contingent is altogether different, and really is just a bunch of horny guys who are bored with their old ladies, and want nothing more than a little male companionship and some good relaxed recreational sex….

> *Do you think many pieces of trade are homosexuals who don't like to suck and are tough enough to act the part of trade?* I think you're on to something there. On the other hand, there are a lot of cocksuckers who would pass for trade. One other thing: most trade, new to the scene, really do want to try sucking and taking it up their ass, if only to persuade themselves that that is *not* what they want.

Do your models like to call you names during sex? Ex-cons are good at this. Usually punk, bitch, faggot, queer. The tapes I make are full of this stuff. It's a turn on. I like dirty talk within the sexual playlet. I didn't like it the other day when a good looking young blonde guy passed me on the street and said, rather informationally than threateningly, "You faggots are all going to die."

In David Hurles, Boyd found a kindred spirit who had exactly the same taste in men and who was equally frank about his sexual interests. As John Waters says, "It was always about straight men…. That certainly was gayly incorrect, and also very erotic in a way that everybody knows; they just don't like to admit it."

John Waters has been an admirer of *Straight to Hell* since the 1970s, when his friend Dennis Dermody told him about it and he bought issues at Gay Treasures. For John, the signal virtue of those early issues is that "they're not campy. They're warped. They are shocking because they're almost as if the *New York Post* did porn." Apparently, the admiration was not mutual. Boyd was in correspondence with Jim McKenzie, who programmed very successful early screenings of *Pink Flamingos* (1972) at the Cinematheque of the University of Maryland at College Park, and who also became a regular contributor to *Straight to Hell*. In one of his letters, McKenzie described the film—it is possible that Boyd never actually saw it, because he often said that he did not go to movie theaters after 1969—and the response was negative. "Boyd said that he did not like *Pink Flamingos* because he thought it made fun of the people in it, something that I radically disagree with. I was kind of just startled by that…. I remember telling Jim he didn't understand. Those aren't real people trying to live like that, believe me. Divine was doing it in drag because we were in a movie."

Boyd must have mistaken *Pink Flamingos* for a documentary, which was not an uncommon reaction at the time of the film's first release. Both *Straight to Hell* and *Pink Flamingos* seemed to come from nowhere, and were not tamed or contextualized by marketing and advance publicity.

They contain none of the customary clues instructing us how to react and reassuring us that we are safe from this filth. The underbelly of American society reaches us in all its lurid glory, as in a circus sideshow. *Pink Flamingos* took the exploitation film genre and transfigured it into a cult ritual; Boyd, the champion of blue collar men and classic Hollywood films, did not know quite what to do with it.

IN "OUTSIDER PORN" Waters reflects on the inner world of pornographers obsessed with trade, and significantly, he gives them credit for being important artists.

> David Hurles's photographs forever scarred some gay men's ability to be attracted to another average gay man. Without these pioneering Old Reliable photographs, homoeroticism in the art world couldn't have existed. Robert Mapplethorpe was a pussy. Mr. Hurles is the real thing....

> Was David also a gay man who could only be turned on by straight men? "I try to avoid the gay ones," he admits, but he's more of sexual liberal than Bobby. "Sure, I go to bed with gay people. I like getting fucked and gay people do that quite adequately, too"....

> "But what about love?" you may ask. That terribly exciting disease that, to me, feels like another full-time job. Isn't love just trying to get back what your parents didn't give you before you were three years old? One thing I learned in therapy is you'll *never* get this back, so move on, for God's sake. Make friends with your neuroses. I know that true love is supposed to be companionship, growing old together, blah blah blah. I thought that was what *friends* were for, not sexual partners! Some of us want hot lunatic porn sex and we want it forever!

(Boyd McDonald/Gay Sunshine/Come)

(Boyd McDonald/Gay Sunshine/Come)

italics ⟶ Photograph by Old Reliable.

Agents for Old Reliable Studios prowl the streets and alleys of Los Angeles and San Francisco and select the state's most gorgeous goons, hoods and whores (for many of them have been forced during the Reagan Recession to rent their meat out by the hour). Note the famous Old Reliable casting couch, which has provided a momentary resting place for hundreds of the finest bare butts in California.

Old Reliable
1626 North Wilcox - # 107
Hollywood, California 90028

Enclosed is $5. Please send me brochures showing what meat you have available.

NAME_____ ADDRESS_____

CITY_____ STATE_____ ZIP_____

Old Reliable ad copy: "goons, hoods and whores."

113

Everyone has his or her "love map," as the late, great, sadly discredited Baltimore sexologist Dr. John Money once called our predetermined sexual types. And we can never really change our love maps, but we can learn to see them coming. A healthy neurotic knows his type can and probably will bring emotional trouble combined with a powerful sexual wallop. But we can see, through effective therapy, that we have a choice. Yes, our love maps may be bad for us but WOW! I won't find this kind of sex in a healthy relationship. So is it worth it? If it is, yes, you are fucked-up, but as long as you *choose* it, you are also neurotically happy. When Bobby Garcia and David Hurles build up the self-esteem of their masculinity-troubled stars by lowering their own in the name of sexual excitement, who am I to say these artists would be better off in a mature relationship of self-respect? Maybe being fucked up is *why* they are so original.

Outsider porn artists throw themselves into their work without regard for the consequences. David Hurles made a lot of money for a while, but his relationships with unstable men destroyed any hopes he might have had of security in old age. And unexpectedly, the circumstances that sustained his endeavor have almost ceased to exist.

"There are still some Old Reliable men out there," David says, "fewer and fewer every year. I wish I could shoot them." "Did AIDS ruin rough trade?" I ask sadly. "Yes," he answers glumly, "that and the internet."

Now that turning one's personal appearance into a striking digital image to attract sexual partners has become a highly valued skill among gay men, the skill of managing unmediated, spontaneous interactions with real people (who might be dangerous, or on a good day, interesting in a surprising way) is vanishing.

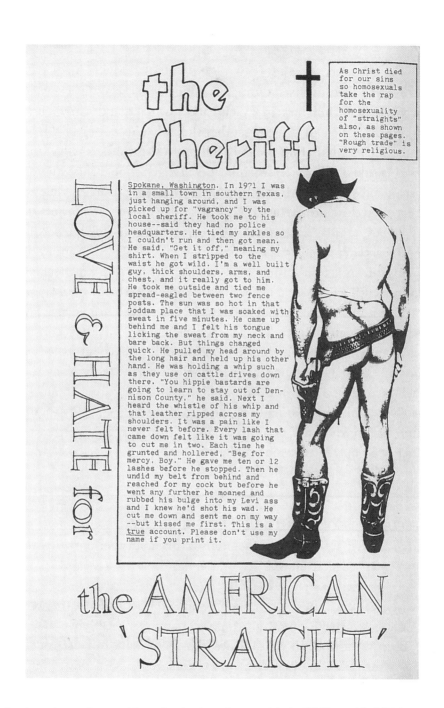

God, guts, and guns: love and hate for the American straight in *STH* issue 10 (1974).

In the introduction to his book *Outcast* (2010), David Hurles specifies how his "type" became fixed during his Ohio adolescence: "There were lots of newly arrived 'hillbillies' in Cincinnati those days, and many felt it was their duty to civilize us 'city boys.' They did; boy did they ever!" He writes with particular admiration for the Hollingsworth brothers, who lived on the wrong side of the tracks when he was in high school. They would pose and strut and show him their muscles, and then take turns fucking him in boxcars or on the railroad tracks. With this ritual began a lifelong obsession. "That school year may have meant nothing special to the Hollingsworths, but over 50 years later I still recall them wistfully and hornily." What they shared was not a romantic relationship, but brief, brutally physical experiences born of convenience and mutual need. These couplings, which "meant nothing special" to his partners, remain vivid for David even in his old age. He can possess his sexual partners in a way completely beyond their control by living in and through his memories, as many of the contributors to *Straight to Hell* do. These men prefer intense, isolated sex acts to the daily routine of maintaining a relationship with a companion. By writing about—or in David's case, photographing—the men they have had, their experiences assume a fixed form and become more real for them than current sexual partners who may fail to embody their fantasies.

BEFORE THE CONCLUSION of his essay, Waters discusses his own sexual interests, which are close to those of his favorite outsider porn artists, but not nearly as self-destructive:

My real type, these days, is a blue-collar closet queen—they're the best. They don't want to go to premieres with you, they don't want to be in your movies, they don't want to meet your famous friends, they don't even want to be seen with you because then people would know. They just want to come over. The perfect boyfriend.

This kind of hookup or friend with benefits goes by another name: trick.

The word "trick" in this sense first gained currency outside gay contexts with the publication of Fran Lebowitz's essay, "Notes on 'Trick.'" According to her, no one would publish the piece at the time she wrote it; it was later included in her first collection of writing, *Metropolitan Life* (1978). A parody and update of Susan Sontag's "Notes on 'Camp'" (1964), "Notes on 'Trick'" takes as its subject the sexual mores of the socially ambitious.

> It is not unusual for the male aficionado to draw his Tricks exclusively from the lower orders. Such a person is, indeed, often attracted to the criminal element. When asked wherein lay the appeal, a spokesman for this group replied, "Everyone looks good when they're under arrest."

The spokesman who uttered these words is none other than John Waters. In the 1960s, "Notes on 'Camp'" explained a sub-cultural phenomenon; by the 1970s, it had come to permeate American culture, a state of affairs for which Waters was partly responsible. Susan Sontag begins her essay with the sentence, "Many things in the world have not been named; and many things, even if they have been named, have never been described." "Trick" is the name of the thing in the world that Boyd McDonald's correspondents described in voluminous detail.

The trick makes congenial company not only for a famous filmmaker like Waters, but also for the many other men who remain undomesticated. They couldn't care less that married couples dismiss them as emotionally immature old-school queens, because they know that couples secretly envy their freedom. These single men prefer sexual partners they can't take to dinner parties with friends or bring home to meet the family.

INDEPENDENCE TAKES ITS TOLL, and personal demons torment the great eccentrics. As one of their number, albeit one of the most successful in recent years, John Waters prefers the open-ended and expensive talking cure to drug treatments.

> Prozac-type medicine saved the lives of a few of my friends....For these people mood stabilizers are a godsend. I never bring up the sexual side effects—I keep thinking I'd rather be depressed *with* a hard-on than happily blank without one.

This blankness also smoothes over a political edge that can make those with depressive and obsessive tendencies fascinating (if occasionally insufferable) companions. The distinction between a political statement and a symptom of a psychological disorder is far from clear, regardless of what the authors of multiple-choice diagnostic tests and representatives of the pharmaceutical industry would have us believe. The politician who can say hello to thousands of people a day and make every one of them feel as though an empathetic and personal message has been conveyed has a psychological profile departing significantly from the norm. The radical seeking to overturn politics as usual once and for all may be in touch with the will of the masses, and at the same time, quite unbalanced.

Boyd's noncompliant politics and mental problems were connected, but it is difficult to say if one was the origin of the other. Billy Miller, while admiring his friend, recognized that he had his limitations.

> We had/have different politics; not adversarial but different. He claimed to be an anarchist—which I thought was cool initially, but I've learned a lot more and wished he had lived longer so that I could have tried to turn him on to Marxism. I think it would have added years to his life, for one thing. All that curmudgeonliness sent him to an early grave.

Alone in his room, Boyd lacked a social and intellectual group to help him understand and express his anger, and that anger consumed him. For residents of Western capitalist countries, Marxism as the path to longevity is not as preposterous an idea as it might seem—Oscar Niemeyer, the Brazilian architect who designed furniture for Communist Party headquarters all over the world, died 10 days before his 105th birthday—but membership in the CP or any other leftist cell was out of the question for Boyd, as party discipline would no doubt have driven him crazier than he already was. The masthead of issue 27 (1975) of *Straight to Hell* bore the slogan, "Libertarian and libertine; Left of Communism," because the editor followed no political line but his own.

The idiosyncrasies of Boyd's politics prevented most self-identified leftists from endorsing his work. In a 1978 article on pornography from the magazine *Gay Left*, Gregg Blachford gives his analysis:

> *Straight to Hell: The Manhattan Review of Unnatural Acts*… is published periodically (over 37 issues to date), has a circulation of over 3,000, costs $1 and is definitely not slick. It is printed by just one man in photo-offset on cheaply colored paper. It has two types of articles. In the first type, the anonymous editor lists the crimes that straight men commit, sexually, in business and in politics. He sarcastically attacks their machismo and bashes unmercifully at their hypocrisy and violence. They are "homo but not sexual," professing love for the women they only use as trophies, hiding their fear of homosexuals in hatred of homosexuals.
>
> The second part of the magazine consists of stories from readers who write in and explicitly describe sexual situations that they have been in and enjoyed…. In an answer to a reader who complains about "too much politics" in *STH*, the editor answers that he "must cater to both those who like to read obscenity (the political news) and to those who like inspiration (the sex news)."
>
> But how inspiring are the stories?

By 'SCUM CRAZY KID'

INDIANA.

It was a very hot, humid night in northern Indiana. 3:00 A.M. and still 94°. And to top it off I was starving for a load of hot come. While walking the streets in search of some horny stud I came upon Jeff, Reggie, & Terry--"straight" rough trade dudes that I bought grass from once in awhile. Reggie asked me if I'd like to take a ride with them and try some of his new pot. I hopped in the car and noticed that they are only wearing swimming suits. Riding along, I was getting super high on the pot and more hungry for cock by the second. In my stoned condition my eyes started wandering around and became glued on the bulge in Jeff's brief white swim trunks. Jeff couldn't help noticing my stare at his groin and said, "What's the matter, faggot, see something you want?" Reggie and Terry started laughing like hell. Reggie said, "Cocksucker, you're going to the beach with us and by the time the night is over you're gonna have come running out of your ears." I didn't know whether to be joyous or worried, not knowing what these guys had in the back of their horny minds.

By the time we got to the beach I was so high on pot and horny from being with the guys that I was slobbering. We went to a clearing. One of the guys told me to get down on my knees. Terry looked at the other two and said, "Hey man I gotta take a piss but there's no toilet around. I'd sure hate to get this pretty sand all wet with my nasty piss." Jeff said, "Man here's our fuckin' toilet right here." He pointed to me.

The three pulled off their trunks, stood before me, pointed their cocks at my head, and began pissing. They were laughing their asses off and yelling at me to "drink every fuckin' drop, you scum head." Little did they know what ecstasy I was in as they hosed my head, hair, and face with their golden filth.

Terry told me to kiss his cock and worship it. He had a big one, uncut. While I was sucking on it the other two cheered us on with comments like "Lick his fuckin' nuts." When Terry's legs started trembling and his cock started going into spasms in my mouth he pulled it out and shot wads of that divine gooey love juice all over my face. Then he took his big strong hand and shoved it into my face, rubbing the slimy spunk into my skin. Then he told me to lick his messy hand clean, which I did gladly.

Then Reggie stepped up and took his turn. "Listen, Dick Face," he said, "I want you to lick my dick nice and slow, back and forth, because I intend to take my sweet-ass time." Slowly I covered his long pole with my saliva-dripping mouth, kissed and licked the fat mushroom head of his cut cock, licked and kissed his swollen nuts, knowing that they held what I was hungry for. Then he threw his legs up and my mouth found itself right on his bung-hole. He went out of his skull with lust, screaming as loud as he could, "Lick my shit-hole." I'd never seen a guy who loved to have his asshole licked so much. Soon he grabbed me by the hair and unloaded spunk faster than I could swallow it. I gobbled it up like a fucking hog.

Jeff, watching, had been beating his meat, and he rushed over and grabbed my head and stuck his prick in my mouth just in time to shoot his load.

I lay in the sand as they all pissed on me again. This was one night when my hunger was satisfied.

PRESTIGE

I don't make any money off of putting out The New York Review of Cocksucking. I just do it for the prestige. --EDITOR.

4

A representative *STH* story for *Gay Left*.

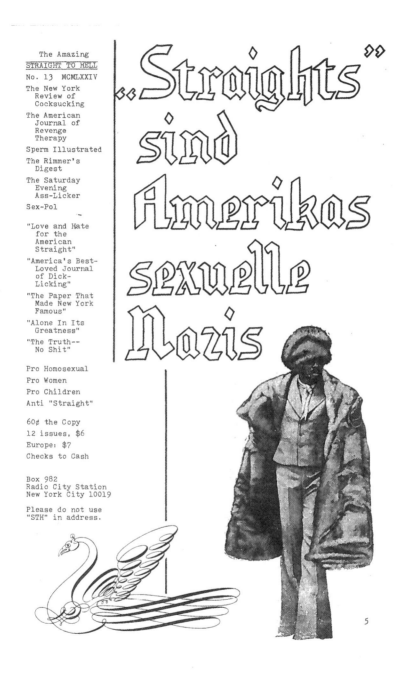

The Amazing
STRAIGHT TO HELL
No. 13 MCMLXXIV

The New York
  Review of
  Cocksucking

The American
  Journal of
  Revenge
  Therapy

Sperm Illustrated

The Rimmer's
  Digest

The Saturday
  Evening
  Ass-Licker

Sex-Pol

"Love and Hate
  for the
  American
  Straight"

"America's Best-
  Loved Journal
  of Dick-
  Licking"

"The Paper That
  Made New York
  Famous"

"Alone In Its
  Greatness"

"The Truth--
  No Shit"

Pro Homosexual
Pro Women
Pro Children
Anti "Straight"

60¢ the Copy
12 issues, $6
Europe: $7
Checks to Cash

Box 982
Radio City Station
New York City 10019

Please do not use
"STH" in address.

"Straights" sind Amerikas sexuelle Nazis

5

Sperm Illustrated: the facing page from *STH* issue 13 (1974.)

121

Blachford quotes a "representative" *STH* story—"Rough Trade" by A Scum Crazy Kid in issue 13 (1974)—in which the narrator drinks straight buddies' piss one summer night in Indiana. He asks,

> Is this liberating? It has been claimed that it offends and therefore threatens bourgeois morality because it redefines "sickness" and calls on us to celebrate sexual behavior as a mutual exploration of pleasure in the human body without reference to marriage, property or "social normality." I question the strength of this claim because it ignores the question of what makes these types of sexual fantasies exciting and, more importantly, it doesn't ask whether we should he challenging or attempting to change these fantasies.

From all indications, Boyd had no interest whatsoever in changing his (or anyone else's) sexual fantasies. Practical attempts to do such a thing—in the US, chiefly the work of the anti-homosexual right using negative reinforcement techniques—have not only involved authoritarian experiments bordering on torture, (e. g., electric shocks to the genitals administered when a subject sees images of men with erections), but have also been completely ineffectual.

The *Gay Left* author acknowledges the persistence of certain gay erotic types but sees contradictions as problems to be resolved rather than (as John Waters does) eccentricities to be lived and enjoyed.

> But we can learn something about the nature of our fantasies by looking at the contradictions that are blatantly evident in *STH* itself. Most of the stories are written by gay men, but a large majority describe well-liked sexual experiences with the same straight men that the editor castigates in the rest of the magazine…. This is a dilemma that clearly confronts us as gay, male, middle class socialists. We hate macho behavior

(15) "STRAIGHT TO HELL" CRASHES THE BIG TIME WITH PRAISE FROM GORE VIDAL

The biggest boost in STRAIGHT TO HELL's half-year experience came in mid-February with a letter from Salerno signed "G. Vidal." In his letter, one of America's leading intellectuals praised S.T.H. as a serious journal of fact and comment.

Mr. Vidal said he was "fascinated" by the story about Bob Hope's homosexuality (issue 5).

"I think your cock-raising style enormously useful at this time," he wrote. "Certainly most of the evil the U.S. has done in the world comes from the false machismo of our fat, flabby 'straight' men with their hard, cold, efficient guns."

He ended his letter with a "Flourish."

Thus, Mr. Vidal seemed to agree with S.T.H.'s main point--that American "straights" do not achieve their sexual identity directly through sex but through the deadly, destructive, and degrading substitutes of war, football, hunting, racism, and other displays of subjugation.

His praise for the paper's directness of style can be shared by all of the subscribers who write about their experiences and opinions for it.

Mr. Vidal's Burr has been No. 1 on the best-seller lists for weeks. He is known to both mass and class audiences: he writes for both trashy magazines such as Esquire and elite papers such as The New York Review of Books. He writes popular comic novels and plays as well as historical novels.

Even dumb people know him through his numerous television appearances. On TV he has successfully taken on such bigoted male impersonators as Norman Mailer and William F. Buckley Jr..

the porcine, epicene abortion fetishist and editor of one of the right wing's best-loved hate sheets, The National Guardian, or National Review, or whatever it's called.

From the narrowly homosexual point of view, in the 1960s Mr. Vidal's Myra Breckenridge pioneered in making the first and most fantastic anti-circumcision statement in a publication for the general audience. Myra Breckenridge's interest in foreskin went to the fantastic length of searching a medical records to see whether he had been circumcised.

Mr. Vidal's main subjects and audiences, however, come from the "straight" world.

Gore Vidal's praise: "your cock-raising style enormously useful" in *STH* issue 7 (1974), with annotations by a subscriber.

and all its manifestations but like it as far as sex or at least sexual fantasy is concerned....

STH, though, cannot be dismissed because it does show us clearly what many gay men's sexual fantasies are and these cannot be wished away. We may abhor them rationally but they continue to exist.

Boyd, who abhorred intolerance, would have been amused (if not angered) by the position of a middle class socialist. He considered himself neither.

Aside from Gore Vidal, who was Boyd's contemporary, the gay leftists of the English speaking world were generally in bad odor with the editor of *Straight to Hell*. Vidal knew about *STH* almost from the beginning; Boyd announced receiving a fan letter from Vidal in issue 7 (1974). His endorsement, "one of the best radical papers in the country," appeared as a blurb on many *STH* publications. Boyd needed Vidal (at the very least for publicity purposes), but Vidal did not need Boyd in any way he could admit in public. John Waters tells the story:

> I knew Gore Vidal a little, and I knew he had contact with Boyd, but he plain denied it to me. He said, "I don't know what you're talking about." When I brought him up to Gore, he looked at me and went totally blank, completely denied any knowledge of anything about him. I thought it was something we could laugh about and talk about, but no, I thought maybe I shouldn't have said that.

Gore Vidal appreciated Boyd, as well as David Hurles (who acknowledged his support in the book *Outcast*)—that much is attested by various sources—but in later years, he seemed to have considered his endorsement of their work an embarrassment.

Boyd's objection to other gay radicals was as much aesthetic as it was political. He never tired of ridiculing their prose, which struck him as prissy, self-righteous, and evasive. A favorite target of his wrath was Dennis Altman, author of the book *The Homosexualization of America* (1982); Boyd remarked that "he writes the way Liberace dresses," one of his strongest put-downs.

In the fall of 1982, *Socialist Review* published the article "Sex: The New Front Line for Gay Politics" by Dennis Altman. It appeared during a transitional period in US history. Ronald Reagan had been elected President, and the right wing was clearly in the ascendant in national politics; at the same time, the moment of American gay culture's efflorescence had spent itself, and its future was in doubt. This combination of factors created a peculiar atmosphere described by Altman:

Newly visible homosexuals, such as those who congregate on the streets of Greenwich Village, provoke a gut reaction among straight observers that far exceeds any objective assessment. Thus the hysteria so easily generated by allegations of homosexual molestation of "boys" despite evidence that the great bulk of child molestation involves heterosexual men and young girls, and where it does occur, "man/boy" love is more likely to be initiated by the boys themselves. (Few gay men have not experienced being cruised quite blatantly by teenage boys; my reaction is usually one of some embarrassment.)

Boyd would not have objected to Altman's assertions—certainly tales of intergenerational sex and teenage sexual initiation abounded in *Straight to Hell*—but he would have expressed them in cruder language. Altman takes up another one of Boyd's favorite topics:

Perhaps it would be easier if we did, in fact, behave like heterosexuals: the far higher amount of rape, child abuse, domestic violence and enforced prostitution in the straight world does not arouse half the titillation and moral indignation directed against consensual fist fucking. In the early days of the gay movement we argued that it was our oppression that led us to having sex in the bushes, the trucks, the baths. The implication was that if society would allow us we would all settle down as happily monogamous couples, perhaps raising Pekinese rather than children, but basically a homosexual version of the TV-dinner couple. Despite the enormous success of *La Cage aux Folles*, which does depict this model, few of us live this way.

Altman's use of "we," taking for granted a collective experience and political solidarity, would have struck Boyd as presumptuous. The passage above didn't describe him or his readers. For instance, they did not link "public sexual recreation" to a state of oppression; they did it because it was fun. Again, the social data cited by Altman could have appeared in one form or another in *STH*; it was the interpretation of these data and how they were couched in an argument that Boyd would have refused. Altman continues,

> If the gay movement is to move beyond a search for respectability, which increasing numbers of homosexuals reject in their everyday lives, it will have to accept a radical sexual politics that effectively denies the claim of many gay spokespeople that there is nothing inherently radical in our demands. This may not seem the best time for the gay movement, besieged by the newly invigorated forces of the right, to defend publicly what not only the Moral Majority but also many liberals regard as degenerate and decadent forms of behavior. Not to do so, however, dooms the gay movement to speaking only for those homosexuals who accept uncritically the dominant sexual rules.

This paragraph, coming near the conclusion of the essay, marks it as a strictly historical artifact. The phrase "respectability, which increasing numbers of homosexuals reject in their everyday lives" describes the opposite of the prevailing mood in the present era of wide acceptance for gay marriage.

To the contemporary reader, the strangest aspect of the essay is that Altman never once mentions AIDS. "Sex: The New Front Line for Gay Politics" was published at the same time as the first Centers for Disease Control report that used the acronym AIDS; it appeared in *Morbidity and Mortality Weekly Report* on September 24, 1982. (The journal's very first article on the topic—about "five young men, all active homosexuals" with *pneumocystis* pneumonia in Los Angeles—was published on June 5, 1981, before AIDS had even been given a name; *New York Native, Los Angeles Times* and *New York Times* reports about a "gay cancer" followed.) The opening sentences of the *MMWR* article tell the story of a plague beginning in America: "Between June 1, 1981, and September 15, 1982, CDC received reports of 593 cases of acquired immune deficiency syndrome (AIDS). Death occurred in 243 cases (41%)…." It continues, "An average of one to two cases are now diagnosed every day. Although the overall case-mortality rate for the current total of 593 is 41%, the rate exceeds 60% for cases diagnosed over a year ago." Altman had no way of knowing the extreme toll that AIDS would take among gay communities, nor could he have predicted its galvanizing effect on gay politics; thus his essay has become a period piece reflecting the attitudes of a very brief moment in time.

"Sex: The New Front Line for Gay Politics" caused a furor when it appeared, partly because of an indirect connection to the *Straight to Hell* anthologies. Winston Leyland explained in a letter to Boyd:

> *Socialist Review* is published in San Francisco once every two months and is coordinated by two independent leftist collectives in Boston and San Francisco. The issue… [number 65] had an in depth article by Dennis Altman on sex and gay politics. The *STH* books were not part of his discussion. The editor of *SR* asked me for permission to reprint a graphic from a past issue of *Gay Sunshine Journal* [a drawing by Joe Brainard] to accompany Altman's piece. I agreed but asked in return that *SR* run an ad for Gay Sunshine Press—the ad in question was for *Sex/Meat/Flesh*. The article and ad raised a storm of controversy. In the subsequent issues of *SR* [numbers 67 and 68] were several letters to the editor, including one from the Boston collective.

In their letter, the members of the collective expressed their wish to disassociate themselves from the article:

> Although sexuality is a highly political subject, which socialists have discussed for 150 years, Altman has ignored socialist visions of what justifiable and liberated sexuality could be. He seems to accept uncritically any behavior by gay men. Time after time he justifies a particular gay male sexual activity by saying, in effect, "We need it for our space." We believe that this is no justification

A Gay Sunshine advertisement provoked controversy among readers of *Socialist Review*.

of any sexual practice. The fact that gay men, lesbians, and straights engage in a particular sexual act neither justifies nor condemns it.... It is a crucial political error to justify any social practice simply on the basis that an oppressed group—such as gay men—engage in it.

With such language the writers affirmed their belief in an authority to which they had to justify themselves—they use the word "justify" five times in one paragraph—but they did not specify whether the ultimate authority on questions of sexual behavior was vested in a political entity, in a deity, or in their parents. Dennis Altman responded that this letter "sounds like a prescription for politically correct sex, which I like no better when it's laid down by socialists than by Women Against Pornography or Moral Majoritarians."

As if in unconscious imitation of the phrase "banned in Boston," the collective closed their letter by mentioning what they called a "pornographic advertisement" for Gay Sunshine Books. This label would have had a dully familiar sound to such authors from the Gay Sunshine list as Gore Vidal and Allen Ginsberg, whose works were condemned as pornographic as far back as the 1940s (*The City and the Pillar*) and 1950s (*Howl*). These were cases of which the collective, as literate leftists, could hardly have been ignorant; on the other hand, their ignorance of Latin American literature must have been complete. The Gay Sunshine list also included Adolfo Caminha's *Bom-Crioulo* (1895), the first Brazilian novel to deal with homosexuality as well as the first to feature a black character as its hero; and *Adonis García*, the English translation of *El vampiro de la colonia Roma* (1979), Luis Zapata's modern picaresque novel about a literate Mexico City street hustler. The collective's accusation of obscenity focused on a mere title, *Meat*—they were undoubtedly ignorant of the book's actual contents—which they characterized as "offensive, politically incorrect, and damaging to *SR*." Had he read this comment, Boyd probably would have said, "That's exactly the point," and been pleased at the power of a single word to provoke.

The Altman article and Gay Sunshine advertisement inspired many more letters to the editor than *Socialist Review* usually received, and most were roughly in line with the Boston letter. There were occasions of unintentional hilarity, e. g., indignant references to fist fucking, man/boy love, bathhouses, and public sex. If these letters were in any way representative of America's political left of the 1980s, they served as a sorry testament to its unexamined puritanism and authoritarianism. Positive comments about Altman's article came from author Robert Glück, who displayed a thorough knowledge of the historical presence of gay men in California leftist politics. He also expressed regret at leftist groups' inability to capture the imaginations of people looking for a sense of belonging as the right wing made popular appeals based on "family, church and flag, in however bad faith."

A letter to *Socialist Review* from Doug Ireland explained that he had originally commissioned Altman's article when he was senior editor of the *Soho News*.

> Unfortunately, between the time I commissioned the piece and its scheduled publication, the censorious forces of multinational capitalism raised their head: our absentee owners, Associated Newspapers Ltd. of London, proprietors of the *Daily Mail*, owned by the press baron Lord Rothermere, had decided to impose upon our lively, radical weekly an aging, bibulous Fleet Street hack as editor to check the "lavender-left conspiracy" that, with the help of some of us, was trying to organize the staff into a union. The Brits used Dennis's article as a club to beat us down. "This is disgusting," said our editor of Altman's essay; "It reminds me of what Winston Churchill said about Tom Driberg: he gives buggery a bad name."

Tom Driberg (1905–1976) was Boyd's kind of gay socialist. He worked as a columnist for the *Daily Express*, a newspaper owned by Lord Beaverbrook, who instructed his writers to imitate the tortured gibberish that passed for journalistic prose at *Time* magazine. Driberg later held elected office as "a backbench MP—the lowest form of parliamentary life—with no hope, under the prevailing heterosexual dictatorship, of ministerial office." Although he was a communist by conviction, Driberg also served on the Labour Party's National Executive Committee; political rivalry was probably the real reason for the "buggery" comment made by a Conservative Party stalwart like Churchill. Driberg frequented "cottages" in London and other large cities and gave defector Guy Burgess a recommendation of Moscow's cruisiest public toilet (where he found a much-desired Russian boyfriend). Boyd reviewed Driberg's posthumously published autobiography *Ruling Passions* (1978), which contained some very colorful sex stories. (One memorable detail: after sex, a Scottish pickup said, "Only sissies like women. Real men

"Only sissies like women"—Tom Driberg visits miners in Kent, 1954.

prefairr male flesh.") Boyd's review appeared in *Straight to Hell*, issue 42 (1978) under the title "An Ideal Homosexual."

Boyd stood alone: he had the independence of a satirist, a sense of glee at provoking people, and a distaste for joining collectives. His politics and his psychology were inextricably linked and undoubtedly alienated him from a wider world, causing him great anguish, yet they were the twin sources of inspiration for his extraordinary publications.

THERE ARE INDICATIONS that Boyd's psychological disorders were far more debilitating than even his friends and family knew. Billy Miller says,

Soon after I met him, Boyd had a sort of nervous breakdown....
He decided to check himself into one of the wards [at St. Luke's
Hospital] and was there for a couple months. I visited him there,
but the weird thing is that he didn't seem all that outwardly
disturbed. He had a very insular way of being crazy. Most people
are demonstrative, but with him, he'd just smoke more and drink
more coffee and just sit there getting more scrunched up and
curmudgeonly. I think he was on some sort of medication when
he got out but am not sure what it was.

A psychiatrist who has worked in the public health system of New York City
gives his (admittedly speculative) opinion on Boyd's condition, based upon
the place he was treated.

He was hospitalized at St. Luke's while most of the addiction
services for the Partners system are at Roosevelt [Hospital] closer
to his home. It suggests that he either had prior treatment at St.
Luke's or that his hospitalization was guided by a belief that he
would fit in better with the lower functioning and poorer patients
with serious and persistent mental illness (e. g., schizophrenia)
than the less marginalized patients at Roosevelt who would remain
more socially appropriate with diagnoses such as depression,
anxiety, addictions or severe personality disorders that more
often follow a path of episodic deterioration rather than chronic
disability.

Even if his literary accomplishments did not require conventional
social skills, the more mainstream measures of success (Harvard,
the job at Time/Life) appear to have continued into his late 20s
or early 30s, which would be very atypical for those suffering
from schizophrenia or schizoaffective disorder. Of course, more
severe addictions and mood disorders can show progressive
deterioration and/or chronic disability. We see such severity more

often when these illnesses start relatively early such as during the teenage years. For Boyd to have such deterioration from a high baseline in early adulthood makes me wonder whether a comorbid medical problem, a lack of treatment, mismanaged treatment, his alcoholism or simple bad luck may have caused a worse than average progression of illness. Of course, alcoholism and other addictions can themselves lead to dementia, delirium and comorbid medical problems that can make a typical Roosevelt patient into a typical St. Luke's patient.

In his last interview, Boyd mentioned that saw both a psychiatrist and a behavioral therapist, indicating that however severe his illness, he was still capable of getting the treatment he needed from the public mental health system. As he said in his 1989 video interview, "I wanted to commit suicide last winter, but that was a chemical imbalance in my brain known as depression…. When I took this drug, I not only didn't want to kill myself, I was glad to be alive again."

Boyd had a positive attitude toward his treatment and took his medication, but his behavior could diverge rather far from what was considered socially appropriate. Billy tells this story about Boyd's peculiar eating habits:

> He had the stove and refrigerator taken out [of his room] for whatever reason, and he lived on a diet of doughnuts, coffee, cigarettes, and maybe the occasional glass of water. I would chain smoke and drink that instant black coffee too when I was there because I didn't want him to think I was a wimp, but after a while I started trying to get him to eat better, which met with a lot of resistance. I'd bring him containers of soup, and one time we went to a Chinese restaurant…. He had so much disdain for any shade of pretension that when the gay waiter came up all perky and whatever to get our order, Boyd was difficult. Then when they brought his chicken dish (the one with that glazed sugary red sauce) which came in one of those metal serving things where

you take off the lid and spoon it into your plate, he dumped the entire platter thing on top of the entire rice thing and sort of startled the waiter and the people sitting near us. I thought it was funny, but I was uncomfortable because I didn't know if Boyd was going to do some other social *faux pas*.

The tendency to act oddly and unpleasantly at dinner was in all likelihood Boyd's reaction to leaving the room that by then had become virtually his whole world.

The drug treatments helped Boyd not only with depression but also with agoraphobia. After his suicidal episodes, he became more mobile and gregarious, and he was able to attend parties thrown by *Christopher Street* and events to promote his books. There were embarrassing side effects—Boyd apologized to those present at his video interview for his slightly slurred speech and gum chewing (to counteract dry mouth)—but the benefits of the drugs outweighed the problems. He was able to participate, if only in a minor way, in a social scene.

THE AUTHOR ANDREW HOLLERAN, in a tribute to Boyd published in 1994, compares him to Quentin Crisp, whose autobiography *The Naked Civil Servant* (1968), the story of an obviously effeminate man in the days when homosexual acts were still criminal in England, was a great popular and critical success.

> For a long time—the past decade, at least—it seemed to me that the two icons of gay life—the logical conclusion, at least of gay life—were Quentin Crisp and Boyd McDonald... whom I always thought of as the real priests of the religion, the anchorites, the visionaries of the desert, each man getting on in years, each one living alone in a room in New York City (Crisp in the East Village, McDonald on the Upper West Side).

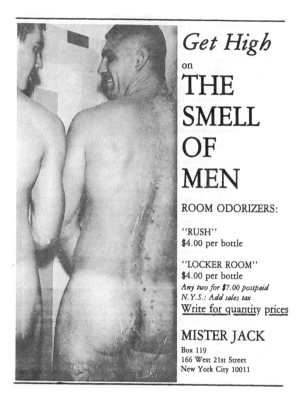

Room odorizers advertised in *Straight to Hell* issue 42 (1978).

He describes their meeting in a taxi on the way to a book launch: "The first thing McDonald said—on hearing that Crisp had just been to a screening of David Hockney's *A Bigger Splash*—was, 'How were the boys' butts?'"

It would not be their last meeting. Felice Picano, author and partner in Gay Presses of New York, tells the story of a dinner party to which both Quentin and Boyd were invited. The encounter was a minor social disaster.

Crisp was as advertised: femmy, overdressed and over-decorated, with puce silk scarves almost matching his long cut, curled high on top, thin, but dyed purple hair. He was a *bon vivant* and born entertainer and he was a perfect guest.… Boyd arrived late, with time only for half a cocktail, and then we all sat down to dinner.… Whenever Crisp was speaking, Boyd had kept up a running undertone of criticism.

When asked what was going on, Larry Mitchell, the guest who brought Boyd as his date and who sat closest to him

> would not go into detail, maybe embarrassed by it all, but he did say he could feel Boyd "vibrating with rancor" the minute he met Crisp and throughout dinner. The only thing [he] had said to him afterwards was "We don't have to wear dresses to be gay."

Crisp was what the British used to call a "flame queen," adopting a 1930s style of dyed hair, makeup, and jewelry with jacket and trousers; this was the outer limit of transvestism at the time, because wearing dresses in public was illegal for men. Boyd's attire was a variation on that worn by the 1950s businessman he used to be. When necessary, Boyd could pass as straight; Quentin Crisp could not, and his mere presence provoked an intense reaction—he describes it eloquently in *The Naked Civil Servant*—the fear that someone so effeminate gives the game away and alerts outsiders to the presence of queers.

In the present era, it is easy to pass judgment on what looks like Boyd's self-loathing and prejudice. Billy Miller points out that he may have had more in common with Crisp than he acknowledged or even recognized:

> Boyd was a lot like other homos of his generation I've met over the years. They all were into Hollywood, and I've known a few with a similar raunchy potty-mouth campy sense of humor. But with Boyd, it was layered with the other aspects of his wit and intellect.

Some of Boyd's irritation may have come from Quentin Crisp's sort of wit. Crisp could be very pleasant company for an evening, but as is obvious from the documentary *Resident Alien* (1990), he had a well rehearsed routine and repeated his best lines *ad infinitum*, without hesitation, and in any social situation.

Generations come and go quickly in the gay world, and every few years with cruel regularity a new trend dominates styles for men. Anyone obviously passé faces ostracism. In *The City and the Pillar* (1948), Gore Vidal writes, "… it was part of the homosexual credo that this year's trade is next year's competition." To this could be added a corollary: this decade's young stud is the next decade's old auntie. By the time of Felice's dinner party in 1989, both McDonald and Crisp had become relics of another era. Neither of them ever revealed their complete sexual histories, but it would be interesting to know which of them had had more sex with "straight" military men, the most desirable tricks—the flame queen in World War II London or the Ivy League fuck-up in New York during the years before gay liberation.

IN HIS LAST INTERVIEW, Boyd maintains that contemporary vocabulary does not properly apply to the men who feature in many *Straight to Hell* stories.

> It was so easy before the gay liberation movement started… because there wasn't this confrontation between gay and straight. All the military were having homosexual sex, and they didn't think about it as such, because there were no gays, no problems of gays going into the service. But now, you see, the straights are very different, too. All the sailors used to be available for homosexuals or anything. Now they're very careful about it because there's a big controversy.

Boyd describes an era he calls The Golden Age of Homosexuality, before the link between sexual behavior and personal identity became politicized.

> Men were having sex with each other but they didn't think of it as homosexuality. And if you would have accused them of being homosexual, they would've been outraged. As a matter of fact, that a soldier or sailor was having sex with some civilian didn't mean anything. It started meaning something very clearly around 1968.

As liberated gay consciousness developed, and some openly gay men found a voice in mainstream culture, a sense of hypocrisy became a political necessity.

> I had to go to the *New York Native* once a week to deliver my manuscript, and sooner or later I ran into most of the New York writers down there. And their writing is completely sexless. But the minute they met me, they immediately began talking about sex because they knew how tolerant I would be. And so I met this guy who writes for a straight newspaper, in which you wouldn't even mention holding hands with a man. And as soon as he met me he said he wanted to suck a Puerto Rican asshole. But you would never know it just reading his work.

Even if they did not exactly live up to the standard of Fran Lebowitz's "Notes on 'Trick'" Boyd McDonald, Quentin Crisp, and the other old-school queens had an appreciation for working-class men, a longstanding homosexual tradition that will never—it is to be hoped—die out completely. As Billy Miller explains,

> Boyd came from a bourgeois background (he went to Harvard), but he had a working class consciousness. He also had that High-Low aesthetic. Boyd liked to call some things "piss elegant" and knew a lot of the old-school dirty camp slang expressions.

Boyd received a free university education under the provisions of the G. I. Bill, which made unprecedented upward mobility possible for a segment of American society. The great majority of veterans who crowded the halls of academia after World War II did not distinguish themselves intellectually; they were expected to assume positions of responsibility in the post-war economy. Only an eccentric few concerned themselves with the demands of art. After Harvard, Boyd faced a choice: to drop out and join the bohemians, people he found too fancy for his taste; or to conform and join the majority, whom he superficially resembled but secretly hated, so he could experience a degree of material comfort. Either way he would have suffered. Boyd went along with the crowd for 20 years, eventually rejecting the American Dream and all its trappings. He became downwardly mobile, and while he experienced a personal sense of liberation, he was forced to rely on welfare and on temporary jobs to make ends meet, a potentially humiliating situation for a middle-aged man with many contemporaries who had achieved success. Boyd poured his frustrations into his life's work, editing *Straight to Hell* and writing essays that expressed a range of class antagonisms and resentments normally repressed in mainstream American culture.

THE MAN WHO IS downwardly mobile—in the eyes of society, educated and a whore, reveling in filth—defies the norms that make for edifying biographies and pleasant class reunions. If he is to survive the indignities of life, he must have a sense of humor. Billy remembers,

> Boyd used his wit like a weapon. He was out to get the oppressors of the world and he liked to hit 'em below the belt. Boyd may have appreciated people like Harry Hay [Communist political activist and one of the founders of the Mattachine Society, the first post-WWII gay rights organization in the US], but whereas they were about writing academic essays that pleaded

for tolerance, Boyd flipped a finger at everything that was false and turned it into a biting joke.

The people of the majority who do the tolerating tend to find the biting joke hard to take, if they understand it in the first place.

An old-school queen with working class consciousness must be tamed for wider consumption. As Billy Miller says,

> Nowadays, the art and fashion world has oddly been an outlet for *STH*, but it's something that was/is not part of Boyd's world. *STH*, like Athletic Model Guild, Old Reliable, Latino Fan Club, etc., are primarily about the working class world. The art and fashion world is exclusively bourgeois, with sex and other things in quotations, as it were.

Boyd was already embraced by a segment of the art scene in the early 1980s, when Victor Weaver threw *Straight to Hell* parties in the East Village. Weaver gave *STH* a "new wave" feel and sought crossover success. Catalogue copy for Gay Presses of New York describes the transition:

> Under the recent change of editors to Victor Weaver, the magazine has become well known to non-gay audiences through public readings and appearances by various celebrities at such night spots as The Pyramid Club and Danceteria, where it has garnered much attention among the New Music and East Side Art Crowds. It's now more chic than ever to enjoy these wild, unedited True to Life Experiences.

Among the features that never would have been included in *Straight to Hell* before Weaver took over was an interview with performer and club personality John Sex, whose prodigious use of hairspray would have appalled Boyd. He would have taken exception to a text characterizing *STH* stories

Cover of *Straight to Hell* issue 44 (1978).

as "unedited," and this may be the only published instance of *Straight to Hell* being called "chic."

Boyd found himself in the dilemma of the cultural outsider: either become an insider, thereby losing the critical point of view and rhetorical force of the outsider's position, or remain an outsider, even if that entails a perverse refusal of hard-earned status. Boyd's social anxieties sometimes dictated his solution to this dilemma, yet *Straight to Hell*'s growing acceptance as art continued. By the 1990s, a new generation recognized it as the precursor of the queer zine, a form that has lasted to the present day.

Billy's statement is ever more true as the art and fashion worlds become omnivorous in their hunger for new subject matter to appropriate, and as the patrons of art and fashion accumulate ever greater wealth. The intensity of recycling—as evidenced in the endless procession of movie sequels and remakes or the barrage of mass cultural references sustaining television comedy—has transformed culture into a collection of ironic artifacts without specific context. Various names for this phenomenon have gained currency since the 1960s: homosexuals and fellow travelers have called it camp; artists and art directors have called it kidding the product; producers call it rebooting the franchise. The process has sped up with the spread of the internet and the infinite reproduction made possible by digital media. In the face of all this, having sex "in quotations" is still not desirable—hence the continuing need for hustlers and rough trade—but perhaps one day, as in contemporary cinema, plastic surgery and digital effects will make anything possible.

Late in his life, Boyd McDonald told an interviewer, "I feel homosexuality is a gift, an advantage." The main advantage of homosexuality in a class society is the freedom it offers a diverse group of people to mingle promiscuously. This promiscuity of intercourse (in the social as well as the sexual sense) leads to myriad complications but makes life infinitely richer. The static suburban mentality—a type of quarantine allowing association only among those of the same class and race—was formerly the province of heterosexuals intent on reproducing and raising families in what they understood to be safety. Now that homosexuals in rich countries have the possibilities of same-sex marriage and adoption, as well as various types of biological reproduction, a similar quarantine effect threatens to rob them of this distinctive kind of social mobility. Those who can obtain everything they have been conditioned to want wouldn't know where to look for anything else. They have no reason to protest and can happily join the ranks of the average. It remains to be seen whether such a thorough assimilation can ever occur, and if the social formation called "gay culture," mainstream or otherwise, will ultimately become obsolete. Modern queers may yet emerge triumphant and figure out how to enjoy both newly acquired legal rights and nonconformist lives. If so, the queers of the future will need a history lesson from the old-school queens.

Men Are Such
Dirty Things

To my mind, one of the best essays about film is also one of the shortest. It appears in Boyd McDonald's *Cruising the Movies: A Sexual Guide to "Oldies" on TV* (1985):

> Unlike so many movie stars, Robert Ryan was able to portray a real heterosexual. But Barbara Stanwyck in *Clash by Night* (1952), seen on Channel 11 at 2 a. m. March 30, 1983, is not impressed. It is very, very, very hard to impress Barbara Stanwyck. She is authentically blue collar in this picture, utterly credible when she says she used to sell sheet music in a dime store, and able to make us forget that she is a glamorous millionaire movie star. She drinks what she calls a "slug" of whiskey out of a shot glass with no chaser and holds a cigarette in her teeth when she lights it. The picture would not be the same without cigarettes; the climax for me occurred not when the director intended it but earlier in the picture when Ryan, fairly tough himself but of course no match for Stanwyck, lit two cigarettes and handed one

to her. She accepted it but looked at it with an easy, graceful scorn for just a fraction of a second and tossed it over her shoulder. I was so shocked I didn't notice what Ryan did. I believe he did nothing; what could he do?

Boyd reads *Clash by Night* against the grain. He has little concern for the director's intentions, the forward motion of the plot, the sense of an ending, or any of the other things holding conventional film criticism together. Like a latter-day Surrealist, he wrests a single moment from a film, but he expands upon it lucidly rather than deliriously. His approach poses a radical question challenging the coherence that an army of studio employees works very hard to maintain: does the audience consume a movie's plot as it is expected to, or does it look for throwaway gestures that reveal a greater truth?

Boyd makes a whole world available to us in a short text, 200 words long, or less than one typed page in manuscript. That world is his own, and in the essay he reveals a few bits of autobiography. Boyd did not see this movie at a revival house, but on television. He stayed up most of the night, almost certainly alone in his room chain smoking, poring over the details of a 30 year old movie, an "oldie" broadcast not on a network channel or public television, but on a "blue collar" channel at the edge of the dial. He identifies with the poor and working classes; by his lights, the main virtue of Barbara Stanwyck's performance is that she can "make us forget that she is a glamorous millionaire movie star." He craves a proletarian authenticity, and this craving has an erotic edge. About the male lead, Robert Ryan, Boyd concedes only that he "was able to portray a real heterosexual." The essay alludes to the sexual appeal of the straight man (as opposed to the man who pretends to be straight and fails), but the main attraction is Barbara Stanwyck, who overpowers Robert Ryan, leaving him speechless and unable to act—"what could he do?"—in the face of her "easy, graceful scorn." For Boyd, even a strong man is no match for a strong woman.

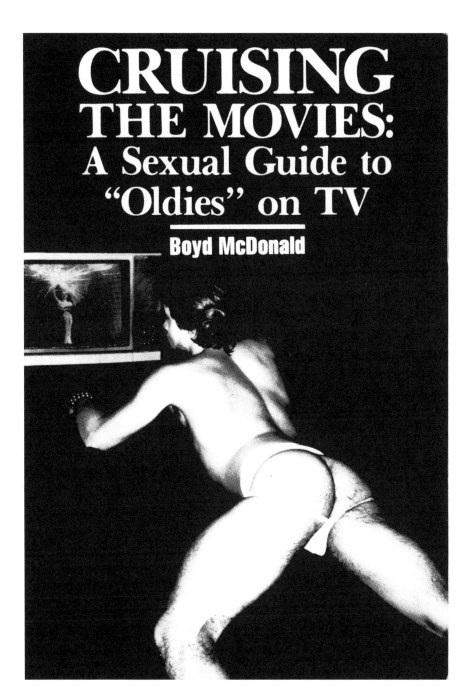

Watching TV bareassed: the cover of the first edition of *Cruising the Movies* (1985).

STRAIGHT TO HELL's insistent focus on "true homosexual experiences" reminds me of the passage in Juan Goytisolo's autobiography *Forbidden Territory* (1985) describing the first time he met Jean Genet:

> Suddenly he turns to me and asks point-blank:
>
> "What about you? Are you a queer?"
>
> In my confusion, I reply that I have had homosexual experiences— something that until then I had never revealed in public… I suppose I blushed when I answered—makes no impression on him at all.
>
> "Experiences! Everybody has had experiences! You talk like an Anglo-Saxon pederast! I meant dreams, desires, fantasies."

For almost anyone born and raised in the 20th Century, the phrase "dreams, desires, fantasies" conjures an association with the movies, and that locus of fantasy *par excellence*, the movie star.

The phenomenon of the star arose spontaneously "from below" among popular audiences during the second decade of the 20th Century. Up until that point, producers, unaware of the commercial potential of actors as personalities and afraid that they would demand too much money, had used performers without credit. As Kenneth Anger describes it, when

> crowds all over the country seemed to be flocking to see favorite performers known only as "Little Mary," "The Biograph Boy," or "The Vitagraph Girl," the disdained actors, until then thought of as little more than hired help, suddenly acquired ticket-selling importance. The already-famous faces took on names and rapidly-rising salaries: the Star System—a decidedly mixed blessing—was born.

There was more to the star than economics; there was a religious aspect to the phenomenon as well. Anger calls the early movie palaces "Wonder Sanctuaries where millions worshipped," and the development of cults (aided by the studios' publicity departments) as "this novel and pagan religion." The choice of the word "pagan" is not an idle one. The movie gods (always plural) appealed to their devotees in ways that harkened back to the Greek gods, who were worshiped in ecstatic rituals, who possessed human passions like anger, lust, and jealousy, and who acted on those passions capriciously.

In his French translation (more of an adaptation) of the Reverend George W. Cox's *Manual of Mythology* (1868), Stéphane Mallarmé made a significant change. He wrote, "Si les dieux ne font rien d'inconvenant, c'est alors qu'ils ne sont plus dieux du tout"—in English, "If the gods do nothing unseemly, then they are no longer gods at all." The original text reads, "If the gods do aught unseemly, then they are not gods at all." (This sentence is itself a translation from Euripides.) It is possible that Mallarmé understood the English word "aught" to mean "nothing" rather than its dictionary meaning of "anything." It is also possible that the typesetter changed the text to its opposite, or that Mallarmé, obsessive that he was, made this subversive revision on purpose. If so,

> Twenty-five centuries of morality—pagan, Christian, and secular—seem to fall away before these words. Can it be, then, that in order to be a god one *must* be involved in unseemly behavior? Can it be that that vast repertoire of unnamable acts as come across in the ancient fables is itself the code through which the gods make themselves manifest? Such a theological vision would demand long and considered reflection.

Roberto Calasso raises these questions in his book *Literature and the Gods* (2001). Mallarmé died in 1898; he did not live to see the development of movie star cults and the gilded excesses of the silent era. Yet this idea, that gods are worshipped not because they are perfect but because they embody human failings on a superhuman scale, would have a great future in the minds of the credulous in the US, a predominantly monotheistic, Judeo-Christian culture. With the success of the movies, a bunch of former proletarians who had skill in pantomime, pretty faces, and impressive physical endowments were elevated to god-like status, and suddenly deemed capable, just by setting a bad example, of toppling centuries of morality.

DURING THE EARLY 1920s, scandals involving actors cracking up and misbehaving caused periodic public relations crises for movie studios with investments of millions of dollars to lose. Kenneth Anger colorfully describes the reaction to revelations about the lurid personal lives of stars: "Professional do-gooders would brand Hollywood a New Babylon whose evil influence rivaled the legendary depravity of old." The film industry's response was to form the Motion Picture Producers and Distributors of America, and to appoint someone to oversee Hollywood's public morality. The producers chose Will Hays, who was the Postmaster General of President Warren G. Harding's famously corrupt administration, and who, like most of the Harding cabinet, had been implicated in the Teapot Dome scandal. Hays was paid $100,000 a year, and earned his salary by placating concerned citizens while the producers did more or less whatever they wished for the rest of the decade.

In 1930, the Motion Picture Producers and Distributors of America adopted the Motion Picture Production Code, which was enforced from 1934 until 1968, when it was abandoned in favor of the MPAA ratings system currently in use. These rules were the guidelines by which the film industry policed itself, and thereby circumvented formal US Government censorship.

The premise that if corrupt people make movies, then these movies will corrupt their audiences, with an underlying insistence on a Christian notion of evil, finds florid expression in the prose of a Jesuit priest named Daniel Aloysius Lord.

Art can be morally evil in its effects. This is the case clearly enough with unclean art, indecent books, suggestive drama. The effect on the lives of men and women are [sic] obvious.

Note: It has often been argued that art itself is unmoral, neither good nor bad. This is true of the THING which is music, painting, poetry, etc. But the THING is the PRODUCT of some person's mind, and the intention of that mind was either good or bad morally when it produced the thing. Besides, the thing has its EFFECT upon those who come into contact with it. In both these ways, that is, as a product of a mind and as the cause of definite effects, it has a deep moral significance and unmistakable moral quality.

This passage comes from Lord's major work, the original version of the Production Code dating from 1930. Lord wrote it with help from Martin Quigley, publisher of the *Motion Picture Herald*, and Cardinal Mundelein of Chicago. Producers accepted the text of the Code almost unedited. (For instance, they retained the repeated use of all capital letters, which suggests condescension to the reader.) Lord was a well-known Catholic writer who also edited a publication called *The Queen's Work*. His superior in the church had a rather lurid personal life and is mentioned in a submission "from a priest" published in *Meat*:

At the death of George Mundelein, Cardinal Archbishop of Chicago from 1915 to 1939, four cops were needed to eject the harem of bumboys which His Eminence had lodging right there in his palace with him.

There is no further description of the bumboys. The rest of the text concerns the loss of jewelry, such as a heavy gold and amethyst ring stolen from the Bishop of Worcester, Massachusetts, and pawned by a young Marine; another episcopal ring was flushed down the toilet.

The Production Code declared vast areas of human experience, including bumboys and toilets, off limits to American movies. The proscriptions most pertinent to Boyd McDonald's later work included the following:

—The sanctity of the institution of marriage and the home shall be upheld.
—Pictures shall not infer that low forms of sex relationship are the accepted or common thing....
—Sex perversion or any inference to it is forbidden....
—Miscegenation (sex relationships between the white and black races) is forbidden....
—Certain places are so closely and thoroughly associated with sexual life or with sexual sin that their use must be carefully limited.

Regarding the penultimate item on the list, Boyd reminds us in *Scum* that "black and white men were sexually integrated long before this nation integrated them in schools and jobs." The phrase "certain places" in the last item was generally understood to mean brothels and the offices of abortion doctors. Lord may have had other locales in mind as well, places mentioned in the pages of *Straight to Hell*, e. g., public toilets, parks, locker rooms, and even the palaces of the Catholic Church's hierarchy. All were possible venues for the queen's work.

THE PRODUCTION CODE was decisive in shaping the consciousness of generations of movie fans—a large proportion of the US population in the days before television—and Boyd McDonald was no exception. These "Don'ts and Be Carefuls" were promulgated in an attempt to control public discourse from the year Boyd entered elementary school (1930) until the year he left the workplace (1968). Later, the Production Code and the assumptions behind it defined the targets of Boyd's satirical writing, whether the subject was a film or not. Especially important to him were two related effects of the restrictions on popular cinema: first, the homosexual was obliged to construct a life for himself without the aid of self-affirming images; and second, the benighted were lulled into a complacency untroubled by the existence of the homosexual. Men had sex with each other constantly without anyone but the interested parties—including "dirt" (vice cops) and the occasional "do-gooder"—paying attention. When these men went to the movies, they had little expectation of seeing anyone resembling themselves, so in the absence of actors going after cock, homosexual fantasies revolved around actresses who could go after men (if not their cocks) as enthusiastically as the Production Code would allow them.

In the context of a review of Pauline Kael's *5001 Nights at the Movies* (1982) called "A Hearty Heterosexual Looks at the Picture Biz," Boyd explicitly presents his point of view as a writer about film. He also expresses his preference for actresses, and reveals something about his viewing habits.

In fact Kael is the only real man, in the classical sense, among the huge mob of picture reviewers (or as they prefer, film critics) in New York. She is typically heterosexual in her frequent, and suspect, use of the adjective "bitchy" to depict women, and shows no awareness that it is boys and men who are the real bitches in our culture; the entire cast of *The Women*, who after all restrict their fighting to people they know, do not add up to anything as "bitchy" as a single sexually-distressed boy or man who calls a perfect stranger "fag."

Motion pictures are for people who like to watch women; the men in pictures, as Bette Davis and Kael herself have said, are not *men*. There's better stuff on the streets, any street; the streets are my cinema, the male whores my Brandos of the boulevard, the only time I see on the streets men like those who appear in pictures—Warren Beatty, Ronnie Reagan, Robert Taylor, Ryan O'Neal, Robert Redford and so on—is when by coincidence I pass, just as it is letting out, a dancing school. I haven't gone to the movies since 1969 (*The Damned*); that picture, according to Kael, has "gorgeous naked boys in black lace panties," an observation that, if it had appeared in any other magazine, could be reprinted… as its "Neatest Trick of the Week." But I watch oldies on TV.

Thus Boyd McDonald encapsulates the inspiration for his own book, *Cruising the Movies*.

IN *CRUISING THE MOVIES*, Boyd scrutinizes the anatomy of Ronald and Nancy Reagan with maniacal glee. The President is not only flabby and "sloppy assed," but also has tits and wears more makeup than Lucille Ball. In an essay on *John Loves Mary* (1949), Boyd writes mainly about Reagan's curiously feminine legs, and speculates that this display of flesh—he appears in the movie without pants not once but twice—is proof of the existence of heterosexuality in Hollywood. A homosexual would not have allowed such a casting error to occur. Reagan's lack of masculine attributes caused him to lash out at men whom he perceived (or, more likely, whom his speechwriters and handlers perceived) to be less than men, the homosexuals. The First Lady, a hard and remorseless political creature, exuded a skeletal and artificial femininity; she stayed thin by living on grapes and regularly flew a California manicurist to the White House to apply five coats of polish to her fingernails. In response to Kenneth Anger's claim that he had obtained a photograph of Mrs. Reagan's "twat" (taken back when she was Nancy Davis), Boyd asks to hear from any reader who has a picture of her "butt-hole."

These sorts of barbs, once common, are no longer much heard among cinema spectators, now that "oldies," which had formerly served as cheap programming for revival houses and independent television stations, have been elevated to serious archive screenings and expensive cable channels, where the odor of sanctity clings to them. Going to movies is not the collective ritual it once was, and internet blogs, written by lone spectators, are hardly an adequate replacement for spontaneous audience participation.

Recent attempts to rehabilitate Reagan's image—"he wasn't as bad as the Bushes," et cetera—cry out for renewed expressions of irreverence and further reminders that there was a time when, as Boyd told an interviewer, "It was shocking to have people like Nixon and Reagan in minor offices, let alone President." Furthermore, there was a time when it was shocking for a second-rate actor to have a successful political career.

THE ACTORS APPEARING in films interested Boyd much more than the people working behind the camera. He belonged to an old-fashioned generation of film fans who populated the audiences of revival houses and special screenings around New York. In a *Village Voice* article from 1975, Mark Jacobson describes what he calls a "film freak":

> Tad is a Bette Davis fan. He got his hair rinsed blonde and sometimes he uses a curling iron on it. He walks with his hand in his back pocket. He says "what a dump" a lot. He also spends at least 15 hours a week watching movies…. Tad usually can be seen at any Bette movie at the Theatre 80 St. Marks, or MoMA, or in front of his "erratic little TV."

This form of idolatry—still with us among those who remember Bette Davis and other stars—has been supplanted in respectable circles by a more intellectual form of idolatry that takes its distance from the effusive rhetoric of fan magazines.

The "auteur theory" is an American variation on (or bastardization of) the *politique des auteurs*, the policy of French film critics, first at *Cahiers du Cinéma* in the mid-1950s, then in other cultural journals, to elevate the director from someone who simply kept the actors from running into the furniture to the main creative artist shaping a motion picture, especially one that has a distinct visual style. (An *auteur* can also be a producer or screenwriter, but usually one with directing responsibilities, credited or not.) The original French version was a program of advocacy, a partisan form of connoisseurship, and the critics who adopted it held that if popular films could be great art, then they must have artists behind them. The *politique des auteurs* diminished the contributions of the many other creative workers involved in making movies, and it has been widely criticized, yet has nonetheless proven durable, because it is useful in film criticism. It reached a wide audience in the US when "Notes on the Auteur Theory" by Andrew Sarris appeared in the *Village Voice* in 1962, and what had been a *politique* congealed into a *théorie*. By the time Boyd stopped going to movie theaters in 1969, the movie star fans—in the eyes of outsiders, not especially classy or educated, and very queeny—were in retreat, as the auteurists took over the scene. The auteurists sought publication in journals, programming opportunities, positions in academia, and ultimately, legitimacy for film studies. While Boyd probably would not have had sex with a bleached blonde Bette Davis fan, he did tend to align himself politically with a more colorful element among film fans.

Cruising the Movies conducts a subtle polemic against the *politique des auteurs*. The book includes essays about films directed by some of the auteurists' biggest heroes: Fritz Lang, Nicholas Ray (with *Macao* being the work of Ray and Joseph von Sternberg), and Frank Capra (who has less snob appeal); but Boyd does not once use their names. He acknowledges only a few directors, and all of them in passing. The Richard Widmark quotes appearing in Boyd's essay "Kiss of Death" mention two directors: "Henry Hathaway didn't want me"; and "Otto [Preminger] just didn't know what he was doing." To Boyd, Vincente Minnelli was "one of the swishiest men in Hollywood history." In another essay, "Star of Stars," he calls Bob Mizer "the DeMille of posing strap pictures." Boyd also exposes the *New York Times* obituary of Henry Hathaway as plagiarized from Ephraim Katz's *The Film Encyclopedia* (1982).

DURING HIS YEARS as a film critic, Boyd never wrote about Louise Brooks, possibly because Kenneth Tynan had already published a famous essay on her in *The New Yorker* (a magazine Boyd read regularly) in 1979, and because it was almost impossible for someone who didn't go to theaters to see silent movies in the 1980s. Perhaps Brooks was too highbrow—or worse, middlebrow striving for high—to interest Boyd. She had, after all, made her greatest films, *Pandora's Box* and *Diary of a Lost Girl* (both 1929), in Europe. Nonetheless, Louise and Boyd had a few things in common; for one, he would have agreed with her in denouncing the tendency to value directors over stars, a subject which she, having once been a movie star, approached from an informed point of view. John Kobal included an interview with Louise Brooks in his book *People Will Talk* (1985), which Boyd reviewed for *Christopher Street*. In one of her lengthy and sometimes caustic responses to Kobal's questions, Brooks defends Mae Murray, the star of *The Merry Widow* (1925) directed by Erich von Stroheim, against her detractors.

It's so unfair the way they treat people. Now, for instance, von Stroheim has become an idol, you see, and so Murray just stinks all around, all over. Now, she was the most ridiculous woman, and the most ridiculous actress, and let us say insane. In a way. On the other hand, she was a great success, and anyone who made a success in the business has something, believe me. It is the roughest, toughest, most humiliating and degrading job in the world. So they will not allow her to be even fairly good, let's say in *The Merry Widow*. It was the best performance she ever gave, and it is cruel, when she was an old woman, not to give her credit for what she had: a lovely body, a certain kind of grace, a kind of silly personality. The fact is, her pictures kept old man [Louis B.] Mayer going at Metro for a long time, so she must have had something, for in the end it is the public that matters with films…. It isn't like great literature which very few people can understand and those few people have to pass it down from century to century. Anyone who goes to a movie can understand it; whether it catches them emotionally or not isn't the answer.

Mae Murray, who possessed "a lovely body, a certain kind of grace, a kind of silly personality," with John Gilbert in *The Merry Widow* (1925).

All you have to have is an eye and an ear, to have lived, spoken, felt, eaten, drunk, and so forth.

Mae Murray experienced a brief, heady vogue, outlived her fame by almost 40 years, and died indigent. Louise Brooks nearly met the same fate, but for the support of a few wealthy admirers and an encounter with the film fans living across the hall from her New York apartment. These young men threw a party and used an image from a Louise Brooks film on the invitation, which she noticed, and was very angry until they convinced her that she was not the butt of a joke. One of her neighbors knew the director of the film archive at George Eastman House, James Card, who said some months later, "I would give anything to talk to Louise Brooks." Soon afterwards, Brooks's resurrection began. Like Boyd, she stopped drinking after decades of alcoholism and reinvented herself as a writer of unflinching honesty and precise style. Before she wrote her autobiography *Lulu in Hollywood* (1982), she was merely a has-been. For many years, the former colleagues she saw in public would look through her as though she wasn't even there; only a few homosexuals cared.

FROM THE MID-1960s to the late 1980s, Richard Lamparski made it his mission to track down as many has-beens as he could find and interview them for his radio show. He wrote books based upon these interviews, a series of 11 volumes with the title *Whatever Became Of…?* Lamparski was an important reference for Boyd, and as he asserts in *Meat*, "so crucial to American culture that one no longer uses his first name, Richard." Lamparski is rarely discussed today, because his type of celebrity journalism has become commonplace, and because almost all the people he interviewed are now long dead, replaced in the public's affection by many subsequent generations of celebrities.

When Lamparski began this work, his idea was so new that few believed it had any merit, even though he had no lack of material; there were many actors who had not appeared in movies for years and had no way of reaching the audiences that once flocked to see them. As Lamparski explains in a 2012 interview,

> I had a close friend [who] was very encouraging to me, but he really wasn't very interested in what I was doing, he was only interested in movies, not movie stars.… He said to me once, "I hope you're not gonna spend a couple of years of your life trying to get this thing underway and not succeed… How are you gonna find, I don't know, Gale Sondergaard?" I said, "Well, we know she's alive—that's a clue. And number two, I'll look her up

in the phone book under her husband's name." We knew him because he'd been sent to prison as part of "the Unfriendly 10" [leftist writers and directors who were convicted of contempt of Congress for refusing to answer questions about their political affiliations before the House Un-American Activities Committee in 1947]. I picked up the New York phone book and I see her— Mrs. Herbert Biberman. And he looked at me and said, "You can do it."... And now to get the permission. I called while he was there, called cold, and told Biberman who I was. He said, "Well, she's having a bath just now, but I'll tell her. We both listen to WBAI.... Give me your telephone number and Gale will call you in the next day or so."

Years later, she told me that she was in the tub... and he came and stood in the doorway and... said, "You can go on the air, no commercials, and tell about what happened to you.... So either you'll do it or you won't." She said, "I was never really sure if I had a chance to speak I would.... He forced me into it, and I realized it was the right thing to do." So I changed her life in a way and I proved I could do it.

On Lamparski's radio program, Gale Sondergaard told the story of her husband's and her own blacklisting, as well as the harassed production and distribution of the independent film directed by Biberman, *Salt of the Earth* (1954), about a New Mexico zinc miners' strike. The interview was broadcast in May 1966, and it came at the beginning of a career revival for Sondergaard. While she was blacklisted, she had done some theater acting (mainly summer stock and off-Broadway one-woman shows), but in the late 1960s, she returned to movies, made appearances on television shows, and continued to speak publicly about the Hollywood Blacklist.

Originally trained in the theater and reluctant to act in movies, Gale Sondergaard scored a triumph in *Anthony Adverse* (1936), winning the first Academy Award for Best Supporting Actress for her first screen role. She was the choice of Mervyn Leroy, *The Wizard of Oz*'s original director, to play the Wicked Witch of the West. She made two screen tests: one as a slinky villainess (her preference), and the other as an ugly hag (the studio's). Wary of the effect hideous prosthetic makeup would have on her image as a glamour girl, she turned down the part in favor of a role in *The Life of Emile Zola* (1937), a prestige picture and Academy Award winner that hardly anyone remembers anymore. She followed this role with many others, mainly exotic types. She played a Eurasian widow exacting revenge on the "other woman" (Bette Davis) who shot her husband in *The Letter* (1940), and in *Anna and the King of Siam* (1946), she played a Thai courtier, a role for which she received an Oscar nomination.

Not limiting herself to prestige pictures, Sondergaard did some of her most memorable work in horror and suspense movies while under contract to Universal Studios. As the title character in *The Spider Woman* (1944), she enlivened an average Sherlock Holmes movie, and unbeknownst to her, inspired a little boy who would become an important Latin American writer, Manuel Puig. Years before he began his novel *Kiss of the Spider Woman* (1976), Puig wrote to his friend and fellow author Guillermo Cabrera Infante about his first experience of success, "I feel like Gale Sondergaard in *Return of the Spider Woman*." (This may have been a mistake introduced by a translation of a translation; the title of the film is actually *The Spider Woman Strikes Back*.)

The Spider Woman Strikes Back (1946) features the same lead actress and was produced by the same studio, but otherwise bears no relation to *The Spider Woman*. The plot concerns a rich old lady (Sondergaard) wreaking vengeance on the town her family once owned. She poses as a kindly blind woman while surreptitiously draining the blood of her paid companion (Brenda Joyce) to feed a rare poisonous plant in her basement. Attended by her grotesque assistant (Rondo Hatton), she performs these tasks in a sequined gown. As she pours blood into a blossom, a tendril of the plant

Rondo Hatton and Gale Sondergaard in *The Spider Woman Strikes Back* (1946).

grabs her arm, and she exclaims, "You beautiful creature!" It is a sublime scene in the midst of a numbingly pedestrian movie.

Because she was blacklisted, Gale Sondergaard disappeared from the screen, and her fans were deprived of the opportunity to observe her fade away gradually. Manuel Puig must have been disappointed, because one of his greatest obsessions was locating the exact moment when an actress was at her absolute peak of beauty and allure. Puig did not take a cruel pleasure in describing an actress's decline, because he identified completely with women in movies. He felt deep down that he was a woman, and in speaking with intimates (except his mother) he referred to people exclusively using the feminine gender, which has an even stranger effect in Spanish than in English. He also noted in excruciating detail the decline of his own middle-aged body (male pattern baldness, a stooped posture) and its result:

160

diminishing attention received from men in public. Above all, Puig wanted a husband; he never found one.

By contrast, in *Cruising the Movies*, Boyd McDonald turns his obsessive gaze on actors, or as he calls them, "eating stuff." He holds that talent is not only irrelevant, but a distraction from the main point of movies, the exhibition of beautiful and exceptional people simply being rather than acting. A star is above all a person millions of spectators want to rim, suck, and fuck. Boyd cites the example of Guy Madison. He was discovered by Henry Willson, a closeted homosexual legendary for his eye for male beauty and despicable politics. A native of Pumpkin Corner, California, Madison made his first appearance on screen in the patriotic snoozer *Since You Went Away* (1944) while on leave from the Navy. Madison creates an indelible impression during a few minutes in the middle of a three-hour movie. Wearing his own uniform, with a cascade of blond curls spilling over his forehead, and speaking in a languorous, untrained voice, Madison seems to have been imported from another, more lascivious movie. He sounds a bit like Jack Smith, though he does not ask embarrassing questions about men getting indelible lipstick on their cocks, as Smith asked Frances Francine on the soundtrack of *Flaming Creatures* (1963) two decades later. Madison's character has a sexless three-way, going on a date with a girl and her boyfriend (Robert Walker, in an Army uniform). Before the sort of action described in *Straight to Hell* can transpire, the sailor catches a bus and exits the scene.

The popular reaction to Guy Madison's screen debut, in the form of thousands of fan letters, was immediate. Studio executives signed up Madison once he was discharged from the Navy, but they insisted he take acting lessons, voice lessons, and dancing lessons to become a "real" actor. According to the essay on *Honeymoon* (1947) in *Cruising the Movies*, Gore Vidal had no complaints about Madison's talents, but Boyd begged to differ. He thought Madison looked "tired" in the film, and his attempts to acquire technical skills in acting were a waste. Bill Horrigan, curator at the Wexner Center for the Arts, sides with Vidal on this question in light of the film Madison made between *Since You Went Away* and *Honeymoon*, *Till the End of Time* (1946). "While watching it, I was mindful of the received idea that he was entirely without talent, when in fact, based at least on that picture, nothing could be further from the truth." He continues,

> It perfectly may well be that I'm the only person in the world (among the microscopic sector of people who care about such things in the first place) willing to extend actorly credibility to him; but I feel as though I've spent too much of my life staring at Hollywood movies not to have developed at least a vague vulgar sense of cine-photogenic genius as distinct from its absence. That said, Guy Madison had it ten times over, far more resonantly than many others having more sanctioned pedigrees.
>
> In a way, it's not unlike the Boyd situation itself; if one is willing to acknowledge Boyd as one of post-WWII's essential voices, why not a similar call-out being made for figures like Guy?—and in a voice not "campy" but seriously enough.
>
> If yes, then the Guy-types would be minor variations on the major-Boyd themes; but a major theme is only identifiable if compatible minor themes are likewise being made to feel welcome and essential. And you can't be willing to kill an actor just because s/he never had access to characters on the level (in their own time) of O'Neill or Ibsen.
>
> There needs to be an advancement of the "minor literature" of the movies, one that includes actors whose crime was that they were merely "pretty." The most conspicuous success in this regard has been on behalf of Kim Novak, though she herself practically began that campaign on her own, in *Picnic*, with her character's refrain that she was tired of being endlessly told she was merely "pretty." Needless to say, there's never been a similar campaign on behalf of the male cohort.

Guy Madison, publicity photograph, late 1940s.

Film acting consists of something different than theater acting, something closer to just being. It is difficult to describe or defend in print, but simple to recognize in films. This quality possessed by great film actors can look a lot like physical beauty, and as Louise Brooks points out in her interview with John Kobal, it is easily dismissed; and in the traditional mode of film appreciation, female beauty (accompanied by talent or not) is more commonly praised than male beauty.

Unlike Boyd's rather monomaniacal view of actors, his taste in actresses displayed a range of interests: he preferred women of impressive physical bearing (Jane Russell, Hope Emerson), glamorous antagonists (Gail Patrick, Lynn Bari), and tough leading ladies (Barbara Stanwyck, Gloria Grahame). The only thing he could not abide was a display of mere talent. (Katherine Hepburn was a favorite object of scorn.) He had a special affection for any actress who maintained her sense of humor about the absurd situations in which she found herself. All of the women Boyd admired were adept at delivering a wisecrack, and this ability, learned from countless hours of movie viewing, found its way into his writing and conversation. He did not want to be Barbara Stanwyck, but he aspired to the contemptuous way she treated men, who were, after all, only sex objects.

BOYD'S SENSIBILITY became fixed during his youth in the 1930s and 40s. The models of behavior he observed at that time haunted him (and society as a whole) for many years, if only as standards against which to react. Manuel Puig called these models "the subdued woman and the dashing male." The actresses of the era had to strike a balance between frank sexual interest, which was unacceptable, and complete passivity, which did not hold the attention of spectators. Wisecracks and double entendres enabled women on screen to be less subdued, and they offered the homosexual, whose desires could not be openly expressed except in private, a way of rebelling against convention. The dialogue of classic Hollywood movies became a *lingua franca* for gay men to use in recognizing each other, venting their frustrations, and talking about the "eating stuff" all around them. Among many (though by no means all) homosexual men in the 20th Century, identification with film actresses—their transports of emotion, how they moved and spoke, what they wore—was so profound and complex that few who experienced it were able to analyze the phenomenon or explain it to outsiders. Those who could do so (like Puig) risked being dismissed as silly queens. It was not just a question of strategy or subversion, and the term "camp" does not quite encompass it, either. What was seen and heard at the movies altered the very texture of daily life, simultaneously imprisoning several generations' imaginations and giving voice to their innermost desires.

When the movie studios began licensing their libraries of films for broadcast in the US, the airwaves were flooded with artifacts from the 1930s and 40s. To people watching (and re-watching) these films in the 1960s, 70s, and early 80s, it was as though the glory days of Hollywood had never entirely gone away. They are vanishing now. A publicity machine postponed oblivion until fairly recently, but the future has finally arrived. To most contemporary spectators, the aesthetic of these films seems utterly remote, and the politics implicit in them are incomprehensible. The general address to a mass audience has gotten somewhat trickier since the rise of segmentation marketing and identity politics—two social forces coming to prominence simultaneously in the early 1990s—and any American film with a budget above a certain (astronomical) level must be distributed in so many foreign territories that the studios are very careful about which groups they demonize as villains. Among younger spectators, attention spans have shortened: why watch a feature film when so many other audiovisual phenomena clamor for attention? As digital images, sounds, and texts describing the entirety of human history become immediately available on the internet, the ability to understand diachronic time unfolding, and human memory itself, has atrophied.

A way of life influenced, even engendered, by moviegoing is on its way to extinction, transformed beyond recognition into vulgar new modes of spectatorship; the old rituals are being kept alive in their classical form by a priestly and scholarly caste which must struggle to remain relevant, or else resign itself to insignificance. The old gods have been cast down, and their graven images no longer hold the masses in awe. The artifacts of the original cults—posters, autographs, bits of production ephemera—are lately being treated with something less than respect. Former treasures end up in landfills, on the sidewalk in front of dead collectors' houses, or at best, in cold storage.

FILM FANS develop a solitary devotion, for while people come together at an appointed time to see a screening, the experience of watching a movie in the darkness of a theater isolates them. Each spectator—understood in this case to be a male homosexual, like Kobal, Lamparski, McDonald, et al—sees his own movie, has his own list of fetishes (perhaps not even acknowledged to himself) for which he looks. He lies in wait until he is ravished by the sight of *that* actor, *that* gesture, *that* bit of exposed flesh or suggestive fold of cloth which a costumer or editor or censor forgot to correct, but which becomes an unintended gift to the fetishist. In discussions after a movie is over, the fetishist argues for what he loves above all with his fellow film fans, but only a sympathetic few will ever understand.

FROM BOYD MCDONALD'S WRITINGS, it can be concluded that one of his main fetishes was the hairless male body, and that he admired Asian men. Boyd used an old-fashioned name for them in *Cruising the Movies*'s essay "An Oriental in Scanty Underpants." He ends his account of watching "kung fu pictures on the blue collar channels" with a statement that resembles a personal disclosure:

> In some ways that are too obscene to list here, Oriental men can be more interesting than white men. Many white men crave Oriental meat and so do many Orientals prefer white men; no wonder bars and bath houses provide a meeting place for these two racial types who are so hungry for each other.

Boyd doesn't name specific bars and bath houses or anything else "too obscene."

Further details may come from an unlikely source. The painter Peter Schuyff tells the story of a visit to New York in 1978, when he was 19 years old, in the documentary film about Ray Johnson, *How to Draw a Bunny* (2000):

> [Ray] was still coming to New York at that time, and he took me out for a night on the town. First he took me way uptown in his little Volkswagen to a little bar… I don't know if it was a gay bar, or if there just simply were no women there. It was all Asian men… a very quiet, very lonely kind of place, nobody paying any attention to each other. And Ray was fascinated by this place… just thought this was great.

Ray Johnson and Peter Schuyff could not have been the only white men to visit this bar with an exclusively male clientele. "Way uptown" seems to indicate Boyd's neighborhood. The customers were quiet, possibly because they were not interested in each other; from Schuyff's description, it was early in the evening, long before closing time, so the night's action would not have begun yet. Afterwards, Ray took his young friend to the Mineshaft (1977–1985), the bar and sex club (later a Chinese restaurant) on Washington Street at Little West 12th Street, the place Robert Mapplethorpe described as "the best bar to ever exist anywhere." As Boyd would have summed it up, "Men are such dirty things."

Whether Boyd patronized this particular bar full of quiet Asian men or not, he managed to find the sort of man he sought. When Jim Tamulis called Boyd in the days before he saw him in person (and became aware of how small his room was), an Asian man occasionally answered the phone. Tom Steele adds, "By the time we were spending time together, Boyd wasn't involved with anyone. He was indeed what is (politically incorrectly) called a Rice Queen, so he probably did have some involvement with at least a few Asians along the way. I don't think he ever had any 'steady' boyfriends."

ARTIST HERMITS Ray Johnson and Boyd McDonald were born in the 1920s and died in the 1990s; in 1968, both withdrew from the world they knew as young men. Ray was mugged a few days after Valerie Solanas shot his friend Andy Warhol. Ray reacted by leaving his apartment on the Lower East Side, and with it, his position as the most famous unknown artist in America. He continued his art making and voluminous correspondence from a house in Locust Valley, Long Island, home of the snotty "lockjaw" accent, which Boyd wrote about in *Cruising the Movies*. Boyd saved his life by abandoning his position in corporate America and a years-long alcoholic haze to take up residence in an Upper West Side SRO. He began his own voluminous correspondence, a traffic in sex stories. He saw few people. Even John Mitzel, who knew Boyd well enough to write his obituary for *The Guide*, never met the man in person.

Boyd's horizon narrowed considerably as he grew older. Diagnosed with a severe anxiety disorder, agoraphobic and obsessive compulsive, Boyd could have been completely marginalized, but he remained active and made his mental illness work for him. He often couldn't leave his neighborhood, so he focused on tasks that could be performed within a very small area: his room, the post office, the stationery store. He drew upon material that came to him over the telephone, via television broadcasts, or through the mail. He had a tendency to obsess on small details, so he edited and wrote to an exacting standard and asked extremely detailed questions of his correspondents. Obsession—the gaze that devoured every inch of the male body, the *idées fixes* to which he constantly returned—was the very substance of his work. Boyd didn't need Marcel Proust's cork-lined room or the male brothel filled with furniture Proust inherited from his mother to produce his *Sodome et Gomorrhe*; he had a bathroom down the hall and the coffee shop around the corner, piles of beefcake photos and film stills, and shopping bags full of readers' letters. He continued his work without the comfort of material wealth or a regular partner. The cozy assumptions of privileged, liberated gays didn't apply to the solitary old curmudgeon.

The proliferation of gay bars, sex clubs, and bath houses in the 1970s benefited the young. During Boyd's lifetime, he witnessed the invention of

BLUE DENIM WORK SHIRTS. The sensual delight of denim may now wrap the entire body. A decal over the pocket should say "Chuck." The back of the shirt should advertise a garage. Wash the shirt with a bottle of fabric softener and two quarts of motor oil.

FLANNEL SHIRTS. It is difficult to show off the body in this shirt and it should only be worn when Butch feels extremely confident or is on a date. If Butch should suddenly find himself alone and horny in a flannel shirt, he will go into the nearest rest room and rip off the sleeves.

Clone uniforms as seen in Clark Henley's *The Butch Manual* (1982).

the "clone," a gay man styled identically to his fellows, as the name implies. The clone was an awesomely efficient sexual being who arranged his life so as to have the maximum number of tricks. His appearance was appropriated from the urban working classes; thus even the most effeminate man could look "butch," at least from a distance and before he opened his mouth. While Boyd must have appreciated an effort to identify with the proletariat rather than the bourgeoisie, he wasn't taken in by the simulation, nor would he have participated in it. As Andrew Holleran writes,

> Clones in the Seventies who felt they were beyond the tearoom queens of previous decades (every gay generation considers itself more evolved) were determined to take homosexuality out of the public toilet—and put it in the Rainbow Room…. They introduced their lovers to Mom and Dad, and wanted America to think of them as perfectly normal guys who just slept with people of the same sex. Not McDonald.

169

Furthermore, a significant disposable income, which Boyd certainly did not have, was required to maintain a clone lifestyle.

The dimly lit piano bar, unkindly called a "wrinkle room," provided an alternative for older men with a taste for show tunes and some mad money to throw around, but Boyd had no interest in Broadway musicals and no wish socialize with his contemporaries, either. As Billy Miller tells it, "I talked him into going to a SAGE [Services and Advocacy for GLBT Elders] meeting and waited for him outside. He didn't like it because he said it was just old faggots." Boyd preferred the company of younger men. Paying for their companionship was most likely out of the question, but perhaps occasionally his royalty checks purchased more than just doughnuts and coffee, envelopes and carbon paper.

For Boyd, a solitary joy was the best solution to the problems of an isolated old age. He writes in *Lewd* (1992), "As the years have gone by and it has become more difficult than it was in childhood to find men to molest me and perpetrate crimes against nature, I have come to love abusing myself more and more." He boasted in his 1981 interview with the *Advocate*, "Recently I jacked off almost constantly for five days—except for when I went out for food."

RICHARD LAMPARSKI, another elderly loner, was in his way even more cantankerous than Boyd. Occupied with the immense labor of finding and interviewing hundreds of actors from Hollywood's past, Lamparski avoided self-reflection until he was an interview subject himself:

> I was on a radio program in San Francisco.... There were only a few minutes left and [the host] said, "Tell me—do you enjoy doing what you do as much as you appear to?" and I said, "I enjoy it far more than I could express," and he said… "With that in mind, what is the downside of being Richard Lamparski?"
>
> Well, the question stunned me. I'd never thought of it! He said, "Well, don't you agree with me there must be a downside?"… I

gave it a lot of thought, and the answer was my career had made almost everything else in my life quite boring....

Someone was telling me about the trouble he was having with his car, and he went on and on and on about it, and I said to him, "Excuse me, what makes you think I would be the least bit interested in that?" and he said, "Who the hell are you talking to?" and I said, "To you. I spent the morning with Greta Nissen, the one who was replaced by Jean Harlow in *Hell's Angels* (1930) and you're telling me about your fuckin' car?" He said, "You're impolite!" and I said, "No, you're impolite! I will not have that kind of talk."

He concluded with a statement that could almost describe Boyd McDonald's life: "I realized I didn't need any companionship. I like talking to people on the phone and I have pen pals all over, but I don't really need to socialize with anyone."

BOYD MCDONALD, Richard Lamparski, Ray Johnson, and many others retreated into solitude once they reached a certain age. Interviewed by telephone, Lamparski may be explaining a reason for that when he tells how the movie stars he visited were affected by the ravages of time:

The big question… after I rang the bell, [and] it would open… I would think, "Now, is this her daughter, or is this her mother?" Because they either looked ghastly or they looked wonderful! It was either one or the other, and it was the same with the men.

The faded movie star and the older homosexual find they have something in common: they hesitate to be seen in public. As Boyd wrote in *Straight to Hell*, "They used to say I looked like Randolph Scott, but of course today not even Randolph Scott does." Louise Brooks spent years hiding her face with a handbag every time she left her apartment. "Don't look at me," she would say; but she had plenty of other things to say, and with some encouragement, she took to writing. Those disinclined to literary pursuits can talk on the telephone at little risk to their pride. The old-school queen thus becomes a phone queen.

BOYD CULTIVATED a circle of friends with whom he could enjoy movies without leaving home. He writes about the experience in *Cruising the Movies*'s essay on *Stallion Road* (1947). The film features a shot of a double rear view: the screen is filled by Ronald Reagan's "sloppy ass" on top of a horse's ass. Boyd, without a VCR to record and review this moment, can hardly believe what he sees.

> "My God Almighty!" I cried over the 'phone to a friend when I saw Reagan stick his big butt in the camera, and my friend, watching the picture on his own receiver 60 blocks to the south of me, released a simultaneous cry of astonishment. *Stallion Road*, like most pictures, is not complete in itself and requires audience participation—additional dialogue supplied by the viewers. This is best done at home; it would annoy patrons in the theater. *Stallion Road* is so bleak that my friend and I, connected by telephone as we watched it, supplied not only additional dialogue (all of it unprintable) but also imaginary conversations among the cast and crew between camera set-ups....

> It seemed probable to us that Zachary Scott would discuss with Alexis [Smith] their co-star: "That's some butt Ronnie's got on him, isn't it? I've seen better on a fucking elephant. Shit, he's not a piece of meat, he's only Spam."

Boyd's main companion in this activity was his editor, Tom Steele, who describes their camaraderie:

Back in the 1980s and 90s, I had to work in my office until the wee hours of each morning in order to prepare our publications, *New York Native* and *Christopher Street*. (I was the only editor at the time.) Practically the only person I knew who was still wide awake was Boyd, and many nights I would go to his single-room-furnished to visit. Boyd was a recovered alcoholic, but he kept a bottle of vodka on hand for me to unwind with…. Even if I didn't go to Boyd's apartment, I would usually call him at two in the morning or so, and we would chat for an hour or more. Often, we watched the same late-night movie on our TVs while talking on the phone, and he usually wrote about those movies for *Christopher Street*. *Cruising the Movies* was the eventual result.

Not above a little camping it up, Boyd would also impersonate his former coworkers during these phone calls, and use the salacious vocabulary he so enjoyed.

"Tiffany," I cried in the rigid accent of the Social Register women I used to work with at a small electronics magazine… "Is 'shit ass' one word, two words, or hyphenated?"

He could make fun of his jobs as a writer and copyeditor, but he took the use of language very seriously.

THE WRITER who wants to be published must deal with editors. An editor can diligently help to shape a text and give a writer a more objective point of view on the work at hand or can merely help to enforce institutional power. Many editors are required to impose a "house style" or a standard of decorum, and the wider the circulation of a publication—often, though not necessarily, accompanied by a commensurably higher fee—the stricter

A

the rules a writer must obey. *Time* magazine, ideologically driven and enormously influential, must have controlled and limited Boyd's anarchic impulses in ways he found excruciating. Boyd frequently complained that he wasn't able to write anything of consequence while he worked at Time/Life.

Former *Time* staff member John McPhee spent five years writing weekly pieces with an average length of 900 words for a section called Show Business. At the end of an elaborate editing process, he made final cuts to his texts at the behest of Makeup, the department in charge of typesetting and layout.

> After four days of preparation and writing—after routinely staying up almost all night on the fourth night—and after tailoring your stories past the requests, demands, fine tips, and incomprehensible suggestions of the managing editor and your senior editor, you came in on Day 5 and were greeted by galleys from Makeup with notes on them that said "Green 5" or "Green 8" or "Green 15" or some such, telling you to condense the text by that number of lines or the piece would not fit in the magazine. You were supposed to use a green pencil so Makeup would know what could be put back, if it came to that. I can't remember it coming to that.

In this account (published in *The New Yorker*), McPhee, the distinguished practitioner of creative non-fiction, extols the virtues of removing unnecessary words from texts that writers think are finished, a process he calls "greening."

"Greening" is precisely what Boyd McDonald did to prepare the many letters submitted to *Straight to Hell* for publication. In his correspondence, Boyd never used that word, perhaps because it sounded a bit too much like "browning," an old gay slang term, or because it is the idiosyncratic expression of a *New Yorker* writer who uses other, less colorful words for anal sex. In his capacity as *Straight to Hell*'s editor, Boyd did not put words in writers' mouths, nor did he rewrite their work; he restricted himself to eliminating redundancies. He did not deprive *Straight to Hell*'s contributors of their voices. Unlike conventional editors, Boyd preserved incorrect spellings and odd syntax, which gave a sense of the men who were recounting their stories. He allowed *STH* contributors a wide latitude, and they returned his respect. No similar situation existed in the editorial offices of mainstream publications, so Boyd was able to publish the texts of writers with commercial prospects alongside those of impassioned non-professionals.

Boyd did this work before computers became indispensable in publishing. He never sat at a glowing screen; instead he pounded a typewriter. Changes in any text required considerable physical work, and Boyd wished to avoid retyping whenever possible. He describes the process of establishing a text for his magazine columns in a letter to Jim Tamulis:

> My own little technique for "freezing" my *Christopher Street* copy is not to make a carbon copy, (too much trouble to correct both the original & the carbon), but to make the sheet I'm typing the only copy, the finished draft, which I have xeroxed later. That makes me write more carefully. If I were just doing a "draft," I'd feel, well, I don't have to get it just right now, I'll fix it later. But when I convince myself that what I'm typing is it, I do the best I can. I use a tremendous amount of white paint to change the copy—take things out, put new things in—before I have it xeroxed. I force myself to do a copy that's for publication, for giving to the editor.

Such work may seem like perverse drudgery today, but at the time, his labors had the virtue of being very economical.

BOYD, WHOSE one luxury was a daily *New York Times* subscription, would comb the "newspaper of record" for mistakes and infelicities of style. He pounced on the unthinking, petty attitudes expressed in its articles, as in this example from *Smut*:

Love!—Your Magic Spell Is Everywhere.

"Men and women in crisp, career clothes shared benches with homosexuals, jobless idlers and derelicts," writes Lynn Rosellini in the *New York Times*. I know exactly how Ms. Rosellini feels: I sometimes have to come in contact with undesirables from the *Times*. Why, I always wonder, can't they be more like me?

As a jobless homosexual, he took nothing for granted and relished catching writers acting more like vigilantes policing class boundaries than journalists.

Boyd edited *Straight to Hell* in a way that was not only thorough and rigorous but more inclusive than the *Times*. He said he preferred the uneducated writer to the overeducated one, even though the former writer's texts required extensive copyediting. Here Boyd expresses his appreciation for a contributor's style:

> Like so many *STH* writers, he has that unpretentious patrician plainness of the authentically elite, rather than the fancy pretense of the "one wonders... one wishes... one hopes... one suspects" type of writer, who must pretend to have qualities he does not have and winds up writing the way Liberace dresses.

He encouraged *STH* contributors to read Ernest Hemmingway and William S. Burroughs as models of direct, unadorned style. His ideal was the graffiti found in public toilets. He asserted, "I find men who don't use punctuation are more fun in bed than those who do." Boyd wanted men who got to the point; he could provide the punctuation later.

I ASKED Joseph Modica, who took the striking photograph on the cover of the original edition of *Cruising the Movies*, what his friend Boyd was like. He sent me a text which I present in its original format, in lines like a poem:

Boyd seemed like a very solitary shy person,
although surrounded by hyper-sexually charged
material w/*STH* and all. I think he lived his life as an observer...
I AM A CAMERA.
I on the other hand back then was doing erotic photo spreads...
fucking half the models. As an artist, I felt that was OK
& still do. Boyd I do not think so... very detached.
I AM A CAMERA.
At most he would give a wee snicker at something that
amused him.
Looking over *Cruising the Movies*, I was reminded that several
of the photos were his choices, like the go-go boy in briefs & a
belt, and come up in his writing.
So maybe he had that boy-toy sex for money thing going on,
but I really feel he was more removed.
Total conjecture of course, I do not know.
Now about religion, I'll say, ATHEIST. Religion may have
come up but Boyd was not playing. I'd say that he most
likely thought organized religion to be laughable. Like calling
himself the Reverend Boyd McDonald, of what church I do
not know.
He did not proselytize, but he was secure & set in his belief
system.
As far as political activism: I don't think he participated, but
his work is so UP WITH HOMOS/DOWN WITH
HYPOCRISY.

In another message to me, Joseph described Boyd as generous and modest, and told me that while the publishing business had more than its share of unscrupulous people, Boyd was always completely honest.

Honesty was sometimes lacking in Boyd's relationships with publishers, and his letters to Winston Leyland of Gay Sunshine Press are a testament to

June 25, 1983

Dear Winston,

I want you to stop using your by-line on my books. It's a lie. A double lie--you not only did not edit them, you can't--don't have the ability.

You're in danger if you don't take off your by-line. Put it someplace else, but not on my books.

You're evil, and I'm real tired of you. I'm going to get rid of you as soon as I can; it will be sooner if you ever claim credit again for my work.

Best wishes,

Boyd

This includes new printings of all my books. Just take your name off. *Especially keep your name off the new one (vol. 4 - Cum).*

Boyd to his first publisher: "I'm real tired of you."

his exasperation. Leyland's most egregious offenses were presuming to edit the *STH* anthologies, and worse, attempting to usurp the credit for editing them. Boyd advised Leyland,

> It is a fact, rather than my opinion, that you have no literary talent, and it would be too monstrous a perversion for a person who has an ordinary mind like yours to sit in judgment upon the work of an extraordinary mind like mine. You must learn to be content with your fantastic ability to make money, and keep your hands off my work.

Boyd's letter shows the courage of someone living in such modest circumstances that he has nothing to lose.

BOYD'S CONTRACT with Gay Presses of New York, which brought out two *STH* anthologies, *Smut* and *Filth*, in addition to *Cruising the Movies*, included a provision for the payment of advances against future royalties. When Boyd received his first advance check, he called GPNy. He asked, "You mean I *get paid* for doing this?" Felice Picano understood this to mean that Boyd had never received any money for his Gay Sunshine books, however it is most likely that in this case Boyd was playing a joke on a person he perceived to be middle class. (Boyd also enjoyed unsettling Felice by living up to his reputation as "the dirtiest old man in New York.") The Gay Sunshine Records at the ONE Archives show that valid contracts existed between Boyd and his publisher—albeit much less advantageous ones than those he signed with GPNy—but that Winston Leyland was slow in paying royalties, and his idea of what was owed to his best-selling author/editor did not agree with Boyd's. And yet Boyd continued to publish books (a total of seven) with Gay Sunshine. He also wrote for the gay press, which provided little income. (For instance, *Christopher Street* did not pay its writers at all.) Boyd was well aware of his books' popularity and had an ambition for them to

```
Winston:

        I've removed the things

you objected to (Cole Porter a

cocksucker, Brooke Sheilds's

and Tyrone Powers's shit-holes).


                    -- Boyd.
```

Boyd responds to Winston Leyland's libel fears. This material was restored in *Cruising the Movies*.

reach a large audience, but he was by no means avaricious. He exhibited a certain indifference to finances—for many years he had no bank account—because it was the work alone that mattered.

Unlike many authors who wrote pornography only for the money, Boyd never looked down on sexually explicit writing and displayed no hint of condescension to the contributors of his books. He preferred the word "smut" to describe his raw materials. In pornography, "everything's ideal, it seems like wish fulfillment," he explained in his interview with Vince Aletti. "I'm turned on more by flat reality, even when things go wrong, than I am by the most beautiful choreography. I try to capture the oafishness and awkwardness and all that, but it's hard to get." Boyd's obsessive pursuit of "true homosexual experiences" and his convictions about their importance account for *Straight to Hell*'s enduring appeal, which has outlasted that of most commercialized, fictional pornography.

BOYD TOLERATED his living situation stoically, but eventually it wore him down. Tom Steele remembers Boyd at a breaking point:

I didn't realize the degree of his depressions until one night when he called to tell me he was going to jump off the roof of his building. I was able to get a doctor friend to intervene, and Boyd was hospitalized until he more or less recovered.

It was Boyd's last crisis. Tom continues, "His writing stopped, and not long after, so did his life. I'm afraid it was inevitable. His health was miserable, and he chain-smoked till the end."

Felice Picano gives a precise description of Boyd in his last residence, a place he called "my lovely home" in Riverside Studios. Felice delivered a royalty check, because Larry Mitchell, the GPNy partner who usually dealt with Boyd's books, was out of town at the time.

> From the outside the SRO he lived in didn't look much different from any of the other four and five story buildings on Riverside Drive. Inside the lobby was however quite different; before you could go upstairs or into the elevator, you had to stop at a gated lobby desk and sign in. The gate keeper had a list of tenants and your name had to be next to it, or you didn't get in. I'm guessing that all this security had much to do with the nature of the tenants' more transient acquaintances.
>
> I was given some mail to bring up to Boyd as he'd not been downstairs in "several days." He was on the top floor, his place arrived at by a creaky, industrial-mint-green painted elevator, and a long, two-tone industrial green corridor with many doors.
>
> I was prepared for the worst, but was rather pleasantly surprised: Boyd's room had a high ceiling and a window facing at an angle toward the Hudson River and so it was bright and cheery. It was also clean and neat. The furnishings were as might be expected basic: single bed, lamp table, reading chair, small chest of drawers, and closet door. There was also a closed-in sink and next to it a

portable double burner. A shelf held some groceries: most notably several coffee cans. Below the sink was a tiny refrigerator.

Two things were noticeable—a good sized cheap looking bookshelf filled with Boyd's own books, numbering maybe twelve by then, as well as a bunch of GPNy titles I'm guessing he'd been given. There was an ancient but solid looking Remington typewriter in dark gray and a thick sheaf of white paper. The bottom was messy, that shelf held bundles of assorted looking papers mostly inside Gristedes grocery shopping bags. These Boyd said were the letters people sent him for *Straight To Hell* and eventually the books.

The second most noticeable thing however was tall, blue and white canisters clearly marked "Oxygen—for Medical Use Only." And hanging over the narrow little bed, and also over the lamp next to the reading chair, were tubes with nose and mouth covering breathing devices. Boyd didn't use any of those in the ten minutes or so we were there....

He looked bad: thinner than usual which was already thin, haggard, with deep coloring around and under his eyes. He was dressed casually, and he admitted that if it weren't for the oxygen that he'd already be dead. When I asked him if he couldn't stop smoking... he said, "Well, probably not. I'm an addictive personality, you know."

That was the last I saw of him. He passed away at the end of that summer.... The cause given, Larry told me, was "pneumococcal distress complicated by emphysema."

Immediately after Boyd's death, his sister Dorothy and niece Cathy went through the possessions he left behind in his room. Billy Miller regrets not having intervened to preserve anything.

> I thought initially to try and retrieve his journals and other things, but well, I wasn't in that state of mind then, and I don't know what happened to everything. I should have, though, as he did have a lot of journals and stacks of typewritten things he was working on. My guess is that it all got thrown in the trash, which is a classic scenario for guys of his generation.

There are Boyd McDonald Papers at Cornell University Library; this collection consists mainly of business correspondence, photos, and manuscripts from *The Guide*, plus material relating to the last three *Straight to Hell* anthologies brought out by Fidelity Publishing, which was owned by the same company. There is also a video interview—to my knowledge the only one of Boyd in existence—shot in 1989 by Jeff Perrotti, who was working for *The Guide* at the time. The donation to Cornell was made by *The Guide*'s editor, Bill Andriette. The collection is a fascinating time capsule of gay culture in the late 1980s and early 90s, but it includes none of Boyd's personal papers.

Merry Laporta's special connection to her uncle enabled her to realize the historical importance of his effects, but geographic separation prevented her from doing what was necessary to save them.

> My sister and mother went to Boyd's apartment/room when he passed. I was too far away to be there. My sister said there were many books, magazines and loose papers; our mom tried to go through the papers, but gave up. I'm sure she was overwhelmed. These papers were thrown away. In all honesty, I would have put all writings in a bag to go through later, but I was, and am, and always will be of a different mind.

Over the course of his adulthood, Boyd invented a life for himself. The boundaries of his life were simultaneously more limited (a single room) and more expansive (a worldwide network of correspondents) than those of the family from which he came. He set himself a task in his life—the collection of "true homosexual experiences"—that made no more sense to his sister and niece than a foreign language. The material in Boyd's apartment weighed heavily on these women, and they threw it away rather than deal with the consequences of examining it carefully. These scattered pages contained nothing they would ever need in their own lives, only perplexity and pain.

FRENCH WALL, in the introduction to *Raunch*, tells us that he gave a set of Boyd McDonald's books to his former English teacher, who "remarked that sociologists from far in the future would consider unearthing *Flesh* or *Meat* akin to discovering the Rosetta Stone, a tool to decode true sexual desire, desire almost always elsewhere encrypted by Church and State into phony and hollow statements about 'love' or 'family.'" Billy Miller says Boyd "was punk before his time…. In the 1990s, I started to think that the younger people were beginning to *get* all that and that Boyd was sort of passé, but now I see they've still not caught up to him." Tom Steele, his late-night companion, offers a tribute:

> Boyd was a true renegade and an iconoclast of the first order. Nothing was sacred to him. He particularly delighted in bringing down (in print) political and show business icons. Boyd was also one of the funniest people I've ever met. His wit and intelligence were seemingly endless…. I miss him to this very day, though he's been gone for many years.

Descent into Hades

At a symposium in 1961, Marcel Duchamp delivered an address, "Where Do We Go from Here?," in which he predicted a type of modern art that goes beyond the many "isms" of the 20th Century, and beyond "aesthetic pleasure depend[ing] almost entirely on the impressions on the retina." He made his statement at the historical threshold of Pop Art's emergence and before the tremendous increase in prices for the work of a few living artists. According to Duchamp, the main impediment to art's liberation is "that the general public today seeks aesthetic satisfaction wrapped up in a set of material and speculative values." The result is "a world blinded by economic fireworks" valorizing mediocrity. In his conclusion, he offers a solution to the problem: "The great artist of tomorrow will go underground."

Duchamp never specified what he meant by "underground," but there are two main possibilities: the geographic and the political. The former describes a community flourishing in a specific location (e. g., underground filmmaking on the Lower East Side of New York). Since 1961, this possibility has been all but completely evacuated by real estate development; only a vague aura of glamour still surrounds places where artistic activities once

6

I was forced to
crowd these
two AMG models
a bit, but
actually they
not only are
two separate
photos, but
photos from
two differ-
ent eras.
In the
older photo (top), the
model conforms to
the Victorianism of
the day by wearing an
asshole bikini. But in
the more recent photo
(below), the model's
asshole is covered only by
a bit of fuzz which is not,
if I may say so, altogether
unattractive.

An asshole bikini and a bit of fuzz: collage from *Straight to Hell* issue 27 (1975).

took place. The latter possibility is an underground defined by political conviction and lack of social status, and is subject to a very different kind of external manipulation. From the abolitionists' Underground Railroad to the current generation of "violent non-state actors" (terrorists in US Government parlance), the word "underground" has been associated with unofficial or illegal resistance. During the War on Terror, the latest in a long line of attempts to demonize and eradicate political radicals, any resistance movement has had to develop ever more subtle and adaptable strategies. (Posting on social media is not among them.) Although the word suggests otherwise, a political underground is never defined by a place, but by a quality of knowledge: whereabouts unknown, except to those who need to know.

An artist can inhabit the second type of underground, outside any designated "arts district" and pursuing activities not generally understood to be art making (e. g., sociological writing, outsider porn), operating in a state of obscurity and unacknowledged by authority. The artistic underground (inasmuch as such a thing can be said to exist in societies saturated with commercial publicity) remains wide open, because the cost of admission is dear: the artist's life not as a path to professional success but as an end in itself. To lead this life is to suffer indifference (and sometimes scorn) as one of the undesirables, but at least an MFA degree, with all its associated financial debt, is unnecessary. The sacrifices required would seem to militate against the very existence of such artists; perhaps only the mentally ill can truly play this role. Boyd McDonald was an underground artist and mentally ill, but the stratum of society he occupied has become less and less tenable as the social "safety net" disappears. Only book royalties kept Boyd from utter ruin. Nowadays, anyone attempting something similar would live under the constant threat of homelessness.

Boyd got away with it as no one else could. Beyond whatever cooperation was required to obtain government assistance, Boyd lived outside the purview of the authorities. Inquiries to the Department of Justice regarding Boyd McDonald of Manhattan yielded no results. As far as the US Government is willing to admit, the man who wrote with eloquent obscenity about the Reagans and other political adversaries through the 1980s does not have an FBI file.

A DIAGRAM that appears in Gilles Deleuze's *Nietzsche and Philosophy* (1983) presents in schematic fashion his understanding of the theory of types elaborated by Nietzsche in *Thus Spoke Zarathustra* (1883–85), *On the Genealogy of Morals* (1887), and *The Antichrist* (1888). These types are ideals and do not represent real people in the world, since a human being expresses a mix of impulses and desires, and over the course of a life has the potential for change. At the very bottom of the grid is "the ascetic man," for example, a saint, who in Nietzsche's estimation is the ultimate fool, renouncing everything for "setting up a world-beyond," a fictional afterlife, which is, in effect, nothingness. At the top is the artist, partaking of "the excitants of life," renouncing everything to arrive at a new way of being that is more vibrant and intense than habitual ways, and thereby giving access to truth.

The austerity of Boyd's life in later years might lead some to call him a saint. The resemblance that Boyd's room bore to a monk's cell was mentioned by all observers, and the presence of icons—pictures of nude men taped to the wall above his bed—only reinforced the impression. I would argue that Boyd—whose purchase of a mail-order divinity degree so he could use title of "Reverend" serves as evidence of his contempt for organized religion—was the opposite of a saint. By this, I don't mean to imply that he entertained the notion of evil that animates the Motion Picture Production Code and other religious texts. He lived an ascetic life, but he did so in order to realize his work as an artist. He turned his back on a comfortable life that was unbearable to him because it was irredeemably corrupt. A fancy apartment, a fashionable wardrobe, a panoply of drugs, summer weekends on Fire Island, "the best of everything"—in short, what was considered necessary in the hyperconsumerist gay culture that flourished for a while in New York before many of its participants died of AIDS—these things (and the social aspirations that went with them) were of no interest whatsoever to Boyd. One of the "A-list gays" might say that Boyd, who was born in 1925, had no chance of being in their company anyway, because he was far too old. But what did Boyd actually need in his life? He lived alone yet had no lack of conversation; he enjoyed the company of his nieces and great-nieces; he corresponded with a remarkable group of men, edited his own journal, published books as well as columns of political commentary and film criticism. In sum, he spoke to an attentive and appreciative audience and sustained himself without having to do anything other than exactly what he wanted to do. Decades after he began his project, his work is still a topic of discussion and a source of inspiration. Boyd McDonald is a perennial figure, because he explored primal forces shaping human life—sex, its pursuit and enjoyment—and professed not the dogma of the powerful, but his own truth, the truth of the body.

THE PHRASE "the truth of the body," which befits the eulogy of a figure who died in the 1990s, now seems inadequate in dealing with the life and works of Boyd McDonald. Since Boyd's time, modern technology and the culture of incessant falsification it brought into being have altered concepts like "truth" and "body" beyond recognition. These transformations were underway at the end of Boyd's life, and the media he used—letters (often handwritten) sent by mail, typewritten manuscripts, chemical (as opposed to digital) photography, offset printing, paperbacks sold in adult bookstores— were already old-fashioned. Only with the 2015 issue of *Straight to Hell* (number 68, edited by Billy Miller) did stories about sexual encounters arranged not in public places but via smart phone applications and the internet begin to appear in its pages. Although its rough, antiquated style has undoubtedly been an element of *STH*'s appeal, the interest in Boyd's work is not limited to nostalgia. Furthermore, a claim can be made for him as "perennial" beyond the obvious acknowledgment that men have always had sex with each other and always will.

At this point the discussion, rather than seeking to propel Boyd McDonald into some post-human technological future, will make an historical turn and undertake a search for precedents.

ROBERT BURTON (born 1577) led what he called "a silent, sedentary, solitary, private life in the university, penned up most part in my study" in Christ Church College, Oxford. His existence was austere and monastic as a Classicist and cleric—"I have little, I want nothing." He spent most of his adult life writing and editing a single literary work, *The Anatomy of Melancholy*, which saw six editions between 1621 and his death in 1640. Burton's goal was to know all the books available to an early 17th Century English scholar and collect every reference to melancholy they contained. The resulting book was massive, over 450,000 words long, a best-seller in its time, and still read (though rarely from cover to cover) to this day.

Anthony à Wood wrote a short biographical sketch of Robert Burton and described him thus: "As he was by many accounted a severe student, a devourer of Authors, a melancholy and humerous Person; so by others, who knew him well, a Person of great honesty, plain dealing and Charity." This "devourer of Authors" had practical and personal reasons for choosing his subject, as he admitted, "I write of melancholy, by being busy to avoid melancholy." He pictured his depression as an abscess, a physical object he sought to dislodge.

> When I first took this task in hand, this I aimed at; to ease my mind by writing; for I had a kind of imposthume in my head, which I was very desirous to be unladen of, and could imagine no fitter evacuation than this. Besides, I might not well refrain, for one must needs scratch where it itches.

Burton's mental state was not the only thing he endowed with a physical presence. In *The Anatomy of Melancholy*, language itself becomes an object.

Memorial to Robert Burton (1577–1640) in Christ Church Cathedral, Oxford.

Great blocks of text attest to his sensual relationship with words; for this "mute and mopish" solitary man, it was a massive erotic sublimation, to use an anachronistic term. An anecdote about Burton, first published by White Kennet and often quoted, describes the intense pleasure he took from words. When Burton was depressed (suffering from "the vapours"), he would find joy in the sexually charged language used by men whom later generations would call rough trade.

> In an interval of vapours he could be extremely pleasant, and raise laughter in any company. Yet I have heard that nothing at last could make him laugh but going down to the Bridgefoot in Oxford, and hearing the barge-men scold and storm and swear at one another, at which he would set his hands to his sides and laugh most profusely.

Burton wrote with authority on the many variations of human sexuality; he might have gathered all he knew from Classical texts, but the question of what he learned from the barge-men lingers.

A religious man very much a product of his time, Burton was obliged to condemn the ancient pagans—"Democritus, that common flouter of folly, was ridiculous himself; barking Menippus, scoffing Lucian, satirical Lucilius, Petronius, Varro, Persius, &c., may be censured with the rest"—yet he spent every waking hour he could spare poring over their texts. Burton wrote the sexually explicit parts of *The Anatomy of Melancholy* in Latin so they would not corrupt the common people who could read only English. The device he intended to obscure the obscene passages ended up serving to point out precisely where they were. Most occur in the third and final part of *Anatomy*, "Love-Melancholy and Religious Melancholy." Mentioning an inspection of monasteries and nunneries conducted at the behest of Henry VIII, Burton the connoisseur of perversions makes a characteristic list of the sorts of people who were found in these precincts: "wenchers, gelded youths, debauchees, catamites, boy-things, pederasts, Sodomites, Ganymedes, &c." Burton also describes a notorious Roman emperor with emphatic repetition:

"And no part free from lewdness, no orifice not defiled and given over to shameful lust: Heliogabalus, saith Lampridius in his life of him, welcomed lust at every gateway of his body." Burton's prose, which mixes revulsion and fascination, suggests a remark made by Joe Orton about Edward Gibbon, the eminent historian who devoted his life to writing *The History of the Decline and Fall of the Roman Empire* (1776–89): "What an old queen she is! Send up, send up, send up the whole time."

Almost despite himself, Burton argued for a pragmatic rather than a punitive approach to stemming the ill effects of lust:

> The last refuge and surest remedy, to be put in practice in the utmost place, when no other means will take effect, is to let them go together, and enjoy one another. Æsculapius himself, to this malady, cannot invent a better remedy than that a lover have his desire.

Robert Burton, all desire and no lover, invented a remedy for his malady— the collation of a multitude of voices speaking from antiquity, a storm of language in the vast unfolding of sentences, part hieratic and part demotic, harking back to the compendia of early Christians fulminating against all heresies, seeking to understand the entirety of human experience through one thought doggedly maintained—and all this he did in pursuit of an ideal.

IN HIS BOOK *Anatomy of Criticism* (1957), Northrop Frye defines four genres of literary prose: confession, romance, novel, and anatomy; the last takes as its model Robert Burton's *magnum opus*. The anatomy describes and dissects social types such as "pedants, bigots, cranks, parvenus, virtuosi, enthusiasts, rapacious and incompetent professional men of all kinds." It is the most discontinuous and variegated of the four genres, and it puts forth an argument in place of an overarching plot.

The intellectual structure built up from the story makes for violent dislocations in the customary logic of narrative, though the appearance of carelessness that results reflects only the carelessness of the reader or his tendency to judge by a novel-centered conception of fiction.

The anatomy is a satire that overwhelms its targets by "by piling up an enormous mass of erudition" and constructing an "encyclopaedic farrago." The writer (who is also a compiler) displays a "magpie instinct to collect facts" to serve intellectual ends. Frye tells us that this prose genre, which is older than the novel and may prove to be more durable, has gone by another name:

> The word "anatomy" in Burton's title means a dissection or analysis, and expresses very accurately the intellectualized approach of his form. We may as well adopt it as a convenient name to replace the cumbersome and in modern times rather misleading "Menippean satire."

Frye's attempt to evict the term "Menippean satire" was unsuccessful, owing mainly to translations of books by Mikhail Bakhtin—who wrote at length about the genre in *Problems of Dostoevsky's Poetics* (1929; publication in English, 1984)—and their embrace by many literary theorists.

Menippean satire is named for Menippus (flourished 3rd Century BCE), a strange figure to have fathered a genre of literature. Diogenes Laërtius (supposed to have lived 3rd Century CE, or several hundred years later), in *Lives of the Eminent Philosophers*, describes Menippus:

> There is no seriousness in him; but his books overflow with laughter, much the same as those of his contemporary Meleager. Hermippus says that he lent out money by the day and got a nickname from doing so. For he used to make loans on bottomry and take security, thus accumulating a large fortune. At last, however, he fell a victim to a plot, was robbed of all, and in

4

The Anatomy of Times Square.

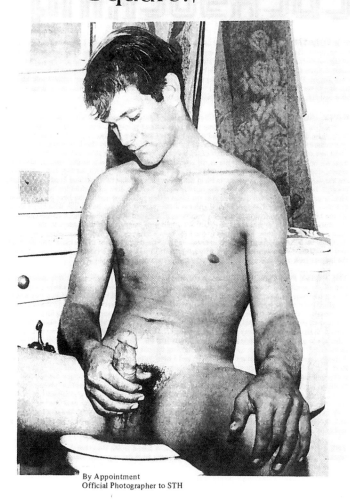

By Appointment
Official Photographer to STH

"The word 'anatomy'… means a dissection or analysis, and expresses very accurately the intellectualized approach of his form."

195

despair ended his days by hanging himself.... Some authorities question the genuineness of the books attributed to him, alleging them to be by Dionysius and Zopyrus of Colophon, who, writing them for a joke, made them over to Menippus as a person able to dispose of them advantageously.

Such stories, which even the author himself hesitates to endorse fully, are essentially gossip, but they are almost the entirety of what we know about an author whose works are lost. In Diogenes Laërtius' brief chapter, he calls Menippus a Cynic.

The meaning of "cynic"—now understood as a person who believes that only selfishness motivates human actions—has undergone a complete transformation in the millennia since the word was first coined. The original sense of Cynic derives from the Greek word *kynikos*, or dog-like, related to the English word "canine." What most likely began as a term of abuse—these philosophers acted like dogs—was reclaimed with pride as a name for the group. The historical record supporting what follows is slender and often unreliable, but this lack of evidence has not prevented the Cynics from being admired and castigated (almost in equal measure) by many subsequent philosophers.

Although Socrates (c. 469–399 BCE) was not the first philosopher, his teaching has come to be understood as a point of origin for Western philosophy chiefly through the writings of his student Plato (c. 423–348 BCE), and of Plato's student Aristotle (384–322 BCE). But Socrates had many students, and we know that some of them had very different interpretations of Socrates' philosophy from Plato's. (Socrates himself gave his lessons exclusively in person and orally and left no writings.) During Socrates' lifetime and immediately thereafter, Antisthenes (c. 445–365 BCE) was considered his teacher's closest follower. From surviving fragments of his writing, it is clear that he had a severely critical attitude towards Plato. His example holds the appeal of an alternative version of philosophy outside the domination of Plato, whose prestige is immense and whose entire corpus of writing survives. *Lives of the Eminent Philosophers* sums up the thought of Antisthenes:

> He would prove that virtue can be taught; and that nobility belongs to none other than the virtuous. And he held virtue to be sufficient in itself to ensure happiness, since it needed nothing else except the strength of a Socrates. And he maintained that virtue is an affair of deeds and does not need a store of words or learning.

His was not a practice of theoretical philosophy but of philosophy as a way of living. There were several key elements to this life: freedom of speech, self-sufficiency, physical discipline, and self-control.

Diogenes of Sinope (c. 410–323 BCE) considered himself a follower of Antisthenes. It is unclear if he ever met the man, but he certainly put Antisthenes' ideas into practice. In the introduction to his pioneering history of Cynicism, Donald Dudley discounts its purely philosophical importance:

> To the student of ancient philosophy there is in Cynicism scarcely more than a rudimentary and debased version of the ethics of Socrates… but to the student of social history, and of ancient thought as distinct from philosophy, there is much of interest in Cynicism. The Cynics are the most characteristically Greek expression of the view of the World as Vanity Fair, and the consequent rejection of all current values, and the desire to revert to a life based on a minimum of demands.

Diogenes was known to have debased the currency, a practice understood not only literally as defacing coinage, but also metaphorically as rejecting the social conventions of his time. According to *Lives of the Eminent Philosophers*, Diogenes of Sinope wrote many books, none of which has survived to the present day, yet stories about his outrageous behavior, which are legion, have assured his immortality.

As a young man Diogenes was allegedly captured by pirates and sold into slavery. *Lives of the Eminent Philosophers* describes his insolence:

> Menippus in his *Sale of Diogenes* tells how, when he was captured and put up for sale, he was asked what he could do. He replied, "Govern men." And he told the crier to give notice in case anybody wanted to purchase a master for himself.

Diogenes gained his freedom then moved to Athens. "He had written to some one to try and procure a cottage for him. When this man was a long time about it, he took for his abode a tub." He lived in this tub wearing almost nothing, eating little, and drinking only water. He defecated in public like a dog, and that wasn't all—when observed masturbating in the marketplace, he said he wished "it were as easy to relieve hunger by rubbing an empty stomach." His contempt for intellectual, religious, and political authority was complete.

> Once he saw the officials of a temple leading away some one who had stolen a bowl belonging to the treasurers, and said, "The great thieves are leading away the little thief."

Alexander the Great, soon to conquer virtually the whole world known to the Greeks, came upon Diogenes when he was sunbathing. He told the old man he could ask for whatever he wanted. Diogenes replied, "Stand out of my light."

Diogenes never tired of ridiculing Plato, who accepted the patronage of the tyrant Dionysius II of Syracuse.

> Plato saw him washing lettuces, came up to him and quietly said to him, "Had you paid court to Dionysius, you wouldn't now be washing lettuces," and… he with equal calmness made answer, "If you had washed lettuces, you wouldn't have paid court to Dionysius."

Diogenes undoubtedly had a similar attitude toward Aristotle, who was the tutor of Alexander the Great. As far as he was concerned, these men, by accepting royal patronage, were completely corrupt and therefore worthless as philosophers. Plato called Diogenes "a Socrates gone mad." He intended this as an insult, but Diogenes took it as praise.

The Cynic, a Menippean satire in dialogue possibly by Lucian of Samosata (c. 125–180 CE), though more likely an imitation of his style, contains a speech denouncing greed:

> Give a moment's thought, if you will, to the gold you all pray for, to the silver, the costly houses, the elaborate dresses, and do not forget their conditions precedent, the trouble and toil and danger they cost—nay, the blood and mortality and ruin; not only do numbers perish at sea on their account, or endure miseries in the acquisition or working of them; besides that, they have very likely to be fought for, or the desire of them makes friends plot against friends, children against parents, wives against husbands.
>
> And how purposeless it all is!...
>
> As superfluous to mention the abuse of the sexual instinct, so easily managed if indulgence were not made an object. And if madness and corruption were limited to that—; but men must take nowadays to perverting the use of everything they have, turning it to unnatural purpose.

Exploitation, conspicuous consumption, and waste have become abundantly familiar to us, as they are now everywhere in evidence. The only parts of the Cynic's speech that strike a modern reader as out of date are references to unnaturalness and perversion and the "abuse of the sexual instinct."

Robert Burton disapproved of "barking Menippus, scoffing Lucian," but exactly what in their writings he wished to denounce remains somewhat ambiguous. It could have been the irreverent attitudes expressed in their satire; perhaps it was the celebration (or at the very least, the lack of condemnation) of "unnatural" sexual desires. The pagan Greeks were indifferent to the sin of sodomy, as it had never been invented in their culture. Burton lived in a time after the invention of sodomitical sin but before the invention of homosexuality. He had the invective of religion but not the analysis of science available to him.

A recent updating of Lucian's *Dialogues of the Dead* (2007) by Baudelaire Jones has expunged all references, even casual ones, to what we now call homosexuality. Socrates is not subjected to gentle ridicule because of his weakness for youthful male beauty, and the legacy hunting in the dialogues has been transposed exclusively to a female (Anna Nicole Smith) preying upon an elderly male. Since homosexuality has become a "social problem," it's best for the writer of limited courage or imagination to leave the question to one side. In the present era, we must reckon with the uneasy coexistence of both notions, sin and homosexuality, and as acceptance of the latter increases, boundaries have been redrawn to impose new taboos. If he lived today, Socrates might be given a shot of Depo Provera to induce chemical castration rather than a cup of hemlock for corrupting the youth of Athens. Over the centuries, the social meanings of sexual activities have undergone such radical transformations that it would not be entirely surprising if one day the phrase "true homosexual experiences" ceased to have any meaning at all.

The Athens of Diogenes' time tolerated shameless behavior and extraordinarily frank speech from a wise man who led a life based on a strict ethical code. Would the New York of modern times allow something similar? Such a person as Diogenes would now be called politically subversive, mentally ill, indigent; toleration, in the best of cases, would consist of a monthly check from the government and a room in an SRO. As the "great thieves"—financial oligarchs and the politicians and central banks doing their bidding—seek to destroy every human value by circumventing democracy, undermining education, enslaving citizens with debt, and telling an endless cycle of lies in justification, the Cynic of today has an urgent message to impart before he is thrown into the street.

Like the Cynics, Boyd McDonald devised no theory or systematic summary of his beliefs, yet he did not hesitate to denounce what he perceived to be false and incorrect in the behavior of others. He sought true virtue, not its appearance, and expressed antipathy to hypocrisy or pretension of any sort. Boyd enjoyed privilege but gave it up in middle age, as Diogenes' follower Crates did. Boyd then lived in poverty in modest surroundings, not exactly on the street, but in touch with the street. He had a horror of the slightest luxury or comfort and kept his possessions to a minimum. He restricted his diet, though admittedly his doughnuts and coffee were somewhat richer than the grains and weeds Diogenes foraged to survive. He became something close to a derelict.

Boyd McDonald may have been virtuous—"a Person of great honesty, plain dealing and Charity"—but he failed in his pursuit of happiness, which was the goal of the Cynics. They sought happiness through virtue but lacked sound criteria for judging their success. The question of the Cynics' actual happiness, in a time before the invention of psychology, admits only speculation. Boyd suffered from depression, or as Robert Burton would have called it, melancholy.

Anatomy's "truth of the body" is incompatible with introspection. Dissection and analysis: the literary anatomy focuses on externals, and in this respect it is the opposite of the novel and the confession. Access to physical anatomy comes by performing an autopsy. Consciousness is beside the point; there are no interior monologues, only internal organs. This recalls two moments in Boyd's video interview: at one point, he criticizes the romantic concerns of the middlebrow gay press—"It's up to its ass in love, so I specialized in sex"; at another point, he mentions B. F. Skinner's course—"We weren't allowed to use any of the words that everyone always uses, like love. You couldn't use any word that couldn't be located during an autopsy on a body." In his popular book *About Behaviorism* (1976), Skinner summarizes his approach:

> The position can be stated as follows: what is felt or introspectively observed is not some nonphysical world of consciousness, mind, or mental life but the observer's own body. This does not mean, as I shall show later, that introspection is a kind of psychological

research, nor does it mean (and this is the heart of the argument) that what are felt or introspectively observed are the causes of the behavior. An organism behaves as it does because of its current structure, but most of this is out of reach of introspection. At the moment we must content ourselves, as the methodological behaviorist insists, with a person's genetic and environment histories. What are introspectively observed are certain collateral products of those histories.

Boyd was interested in behavior and environment, measurements and functions—where men had sex with each other, what circumstances allowed it to happen, how big, and how it worked—but not psychology, and certainly not romantic love. Perhaps Boyd learned a crucial lesson from Skinner despite a poor performance in his course. Another statement from his former professor comes close to describing *Straight to Hell*: "For twenty five hundred years people have been preoccupied with feelings and mental life, but only recently has any interest been shown in a more precise analysis of the role of the environment."

THAT BOYD'S FILM WRITING qualifies as satire is beyond doubt, but this term applies to the rest of his work as well. Boyd used his "magpie instinct to collect facts" to pile up "an enormous mass of erudition" about sexual behavior. He compiled a wide range of texts, from the poetic to the bluntly prosaic, recounting sex in many locales, and thus his publications embodied "violent dislocations" stylistic and geographic. He did not reduce his testimonies to statistics and average them to derive abstractions about social behavior in general as a social scientist would; instead he preserved his material in all its variation and provided only a framework or context to exhibit it. In his publications, Boyd consistently ridicules the lives of the supposed greats—celebrities—and at the same time elevates common daily experience. Boyd's issues of *Straight to Hell*, his paperback anthologies of "true homosexual experiences," and his various columns for newspapers and magazines can be understood to constitute a single vast work, Menippean satire on a grand scale.

TWO OF LUCIAN'S SATIRES, *Dialogues of the Dead* and *Menippus, a Necromantic Experiment*, feature Menippus as a character; in the first, visiting the underworld, and in the second, returning to the realm of the living to narrate his adventure. Menippus brings his "barking" attitude to the journey. While most of the dead bemoan their ultimate fate, he and the other Cynics laugh. Once Menippus arrives in Hades, he sets about tormenting the richest men, Midas, Sardanapalus, and Croesus; the last complains to Pluto that this visitor is a nuisance.

> Menippus: Well, you scum of your respective nations, let there be no misunderstanding; I am going on just the same. Wherever you are, there shall I be also; worrying, jeering, singing you down.
>
> Croesus: Presumption!
>
> Menippus: Not a bit of it. Yours was the presumption, when you expected men to fall down before you, when you trampled on men's liberty, and forgot there was such a thing as death.

In the final dialogue, when asked to judge which of two men is more beautiful—both have been reduced to skeletons in Hades yet seem not to have grasped this—Menippus tells them, "Hades is a democracy; one man is as good as another here." Although he refers specifically to physical beauty, his comment applies generally to any mortal distinction: everyone is equal in death.

In *A Necromantic Experiment*, Menippus tells his friend Philonides what he saw during his "queer original journey," but first he asks what he has missed while he was away from human affairs. Philonides responds, "Oh, nothing new; extortion, perjury, forty per cent, face-grinding." Menippus questions the differing standards that apply to "adulterous Gods, rapacious Gods, violent, litigious, usurping, incestuous Gods" and mere mortals who are subject to society's laws. He consults philosophers, who shed little light on the matter and only confuse him.

To satisfy his curiosity, Menippus goes to observe the realm of the dead, then makes a return trip that very few have accomplished. The place he visits is underground, and he discovers that all received ideas and values are overthrown there. This sort of fantastic journey is one of the most distinctive features of the Menippean satire. Boyd McDonald, the observer of human folly, makes reference to this ancient precursor in the very name of his project. He takes us underground via his own descent into Hades, in other words, Straight to Hell.

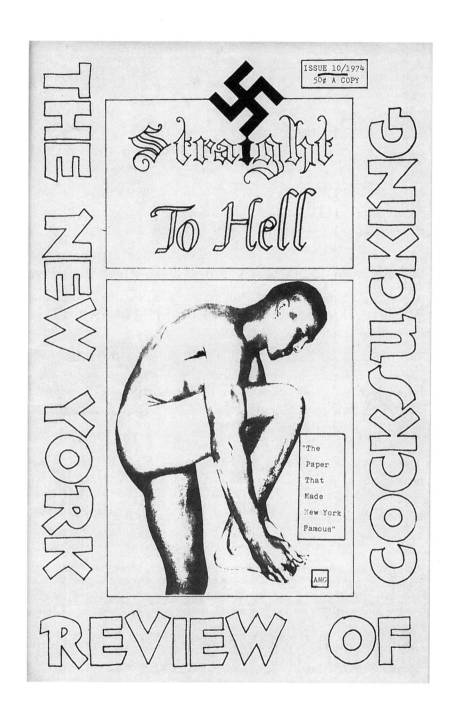

The New York Review of Cocksucking—Straight to Hell issue 10 (1974).

Bibliography

Vince Aletti, "Boyd McDonald's Natural Acts," *Village Voice*, March 25, 1981.

—— "Straight to Hell," *FILE*, Vol. 5, No. 3 (Spring 1982). [Reprinted in *Sex* (San Francisco: Gay Sunshine Press, 1982); and in *Queer Zines* (New York: Printed Matter, (2008).]

—— "Boyd McDonald, 1925–1993," *Village Voice*, October 12, 1993.

Dennis Altman, "Sex: The New Front Line for Gay Politics," *Socialist Review*, issue 65 (September–October 1982). [Letters responding to this article appear at the back of *SR* issues 67 and 68 (1983).]

Bill Andriette, "Remembering Boyd McDonald," *The Guide* (Boston), vol. 13, no. 11 (November 1993).

Kenneth Anger, *Hollywood Babylon*. (Phoenix, AZ: Associated Professional Services, 1965).

Anonymous, "Trucker Uses Son to Lure Kid Cock," *Straight to Hell*, issue 20 (1975).

—— "Blowing the Basketball Team," *Straight to Hell*, issue 47 (1980).

Karen Arenson, "Playwright Is Denied a Final Act," *New York Times*, July 9, 1997.

Mikhail Bakhtin, *Problems of Dostoevsky's Poetics*. Edited and translated by Caryl Emerson. (Minneapolis: University of Minnesota Press, 1984).

David Bateman, "Cum Dripping Fun," *http://dailyxtra.com*, January 17, 2007.

Arthur Bell, "Bell Tells," *Village Voice*, April 3, 1984.

Bruce Benderson, *Sex and Isolation: And Other Essays*. (Madison: University of Wisconsin Press, 2007).

Gregg Blachford, "Looking at Pornography: Erotica and the Socialist Morality," *Gay Left*, no. 6 (Summer 1978).

"Boyd McDonald, Writer, Editor Dead at 68," *Edge Magazine*, December 1, 1993.

Louise Brooks, *Lulu in Hollywood*. (New York: Alfred A. Knopf, 1982).

Phong Bui, "In Conversation: Fran Lebowitz with Phong Bui," *www.brooklynrail.org*, March 4, 2014.

Robert Burton, *The Anatomy of Melancholy, now for the first time with the Latin completely given in translation and embodied in an all-English text.* Edited by Floyd Dell and Paul Jordan-Smith. (New York: Farrar, 1927). [For the lay person, this edition is preferable to the more recent New York Review of Books Classics edition, which does not translate extended Latin passages.]

Scott Burton Papers, folder II.49, Gay Cultural Materials and *Art-Rite* Magazine (1975–1978), Museum of Modern Art Archives.

Roberto Calasso, *Literature and the Gods*. Translated by Tim Parks. (New York: Alfred A. Knopf, 2001).

Quentin Crisp, *The Naked Civil Servant*. (London: Jonathan Cape, 1968).

Paul Cummings, "Oral History Interview with Walker Evans," October 13–December 23, 1971, Archives of American Art, Smithsonian Institution.

"Current Trends Update on Acquired Immune Deficiency Syndrome (AIDS)–United States," *Morbidity and Mortality Weekly Report*, September 24, 1982.

The Daily Plainsman (Huron, SD). [References to Boyd McDonald occur in the following issues: April 4, 1935; May 23, 1939; May 21, 1941; March 5 and December 9, 1942; and April 27, 1943.]

Gilles Deleuze, *Nietzsche and Philosophy*. Translated by Hugh Tomlinson. (New York: Columbia University Press, 1983).

Diogenes the Cynic, *Sayings and Anecdotes, with Other Popular Moralists*. Translated by Robin Hard. (Oxford: Oxford University Press, 2012).

Diogenes Laërtius, *Lives of the Eminent Philosophers*, Book VI: Cynics. Translated by Robert Drew Hicks. (London: Heinemann, 1925).

Robert Dobbin (editor), *The Cynic Philosophers from Diogenes to Julian*. (London: Penguin Classics, 2012).

Tom Driberg, *Ruling Passions*. (Briarcliff Manor, NY: Stein and Day, 1978).

Marcel Duchamp, "Where Do We Go from Here?" *Studio International*, no. 189 (January–February 1975).

Donald R. Dudley, *A History of Cynicism from Diogenes to the 6th Century*. (London: Methuen & Co., 1937).

Jim Dugan, "Uncle Joe" (parts I–V), *Straight to Hell*, issues 23–27 (1975).

Farrell v. Burke, No. 05-0169, 2006 U.S. App. (2nd Cir. May 31, 2006).

Félix Fénéon, *Novels in Three Lines*. Translated and with an introduction by Luc Sante. (New York: New York Review of Books Classics, 2007).

Northrop Frye, *Anatomy of Criticism: Four Essays*. (Princeton, NJ: Princeton University Press, 1957).

Brad Gooch, *City Poet: The Life and Times of Frank O'Hara*. (New York: Alfred A. Knopf, 1993).

Juan Goytisolo, *Forbidden Territory*. Translated by Peter Bush. (San Francisco: North Point Press, 1989).

Stephen Greco, "Straight to Hell with Boyd McDonald," *The Advocate*, September 17, 1981.

Bruce Hainley, "Writing Survey (Part 2)," *Frieze*, issue 100 (June–August 2006).
——— "Second Life: Bruce Hainley Selects," *East of Borneo*, August 25, 2011.

Clark Henley, *The Butch Manual: The Current Drag and How to Do It*. (New York: The Seahorse Press, 1982).

J. Hoberman and Jonathan Rosenbaum, *Midnight Movies*. (New York: Harper & Row, 1983).

Andrew Holleran, "Obsessed," *Christopher Street*, issue 209 (January 1994).

Edward T. Hougen, "And the Flesh Became Word," *The Guide* (Boston), vol. 13, no. 11 (November 1993).

David Hurles, *Outcast: David Hurles' Old Reliable in Living Color*. (San Francisco: Green Candy Press, 2010).

Louis Hyde (editor), *Rat and the Devil: Journal Letters of F. O. Matthiessen and Russell Cheney*. (Hamden, CT: Archon Books, 1978).

Mark Jacobson, "In Praise of Film Freaks," *Village Voice*, June 16, 1975.

Baudelaire Jones, *Dialogues of the Dead: Based upon the Dialogues of Lucian*. (Los Angeles: Black Box Press, 2007).

Hubert Kennedy, *The Ideal Gay Man: The Story of* Der Kreis. (Binghamton, NY: Harrington Park Press, 1999).

White Kennet, *Register and Chronicle, Ecclesiastical and Civil: containing Matters of Fact delivered in the words of the most Authentick Books, Papers, and*

Records; digested in exact order of time. With papers, notes, and references towards discovering and connecting the true History of England from the Restauration of King Charles II, vol. 1, (London, 1728, folio).

Kevin Killian, "Secret Historian: Samuel Steward," *www.thefanzine.com/secret-historian-samuel-steward*, February 11, 2010.

Alfred C. Kinsey, Wardell R. Pomeroy, and Clyde E. Martin, *Sexual Behavior in the Human Male*. (Philadelphia: W. B. Saunders, 1948).

John Kobal, *People Will Talk*. (New York: Alfred A. Knopf, 1985).

Martin Krieger, "The Brain as Gland," *Gay Community News*, April 1982.

John Lahr, *Prick Up Your Ears: The Biography of Joe Orton*. (New York: Alfred A. Knopf, 1978).

Richard Lamparski, *Whatever Became Of…?* Volumes 1–11. (New York: Crown Publishers, 1966–1989).

Fran Lebowitz, "Notes on 'Trick'" in *Metropolitan Life*. (New York: E. P. Dutton, 1978).

Suzanne Jill Levine, *Manuel Puig and the Spider Woman*. (New York: Farrar, Straus and Giroux, 2000).

Ariel Levy, "The Perfect Wife: How Edith Windsor Fell in Love, Got Married, and Won a Landmark Case for Gay Marriage," *The New Yorker*, September 30, 2013.

Winston Leyland–Boyd McDonald correspondence, Box 51, folders 3, 6, 7, and 8, Gay Sunshine Records. Coll2011.011. ONE National Gay & Lesbian Archives, USC Libraries, University of Southern California.

A. A. Long, "The Socratic Legacy," in *The Cambridge History of Hellenistic Philosophy*. Edited by Keimpe Algra, Jonathan Barnes, Jaap Mansfeld, and Malcolm Schofield. (Cambridge: Cambridge University Press, 1999).

Thomas Löw, "*Der Kreis* und sein idealer Schwuler," in *Männergeschichten: Schwule in Basel seit 1930.* (Basel: Buchverlag Basler Zeitung). [An English translation is in Kennedy.]

Lucian, "The Cynic," "Dialogues of the Dead," and "Menippus, a Necromantic Experiment," in *The Works of Lucian of Samosata*, Volumes 1 and 4. Translated and edited by H. W. & F. G. Fowler. (Oxford: Clarendon Press, 1905). ["The Cynic" in Volume 4 has subsequently been attributed to Pseudo-Lucian. A more modern translation of this text is in Dobbin.]

Stéphane Mallarmé, *Les dieux antiques.* (Paris: Gallimard, 1925).

F. O. Matthiessen, *American Renaissance: Art and Expression in the Age of Emerson and Whitman.* (London: Oxford University Press, 1941).

James McCourt, *Queer Street: The Rise and Fall of American Culture, 1947–1985.* (New York: W. W. Norton, 2005).

Boyd McDonald, "Ozarks Haven't Anything on S. D." *The Daily Plainsman* (Huron, SD), September 24, 1942.

——— "Assignment Mississippi: House of No Address," *Natchez Times*, January 29, 1952.

——— "Electronics Lifts the Iron Curtain," *Think*, vol. 23, no. 8 (August 1957).

——— "New Careers for the Handicapped," *Think*, vol. 24, no. 2 (February 1958).

——— "America's Sexual Nazis," *Straight to Hell*, issue 3 (1973).

——— "Hack Meets Quack," *Straight to Hell*, issue 5 (1973).

——— "The Wonderful World of War: Cocksucking in Vietnam," *Straight to Hell*, issues 6, 7, and 8 (1974).

——— "*Straight to Hell* Crashes the Big Time with Praise from Gore Vidal" and "Education: *Timagazine*, a Slow Learner," *Straight to Hell*, issue 7 (1974).

——— "Swastika," *Straight to Hell*, issue 10 (1974).

——— "Art" and "A Kiss Before Dying," *Straight to Hell*, issue 13 (1974).

——— "Artist Likes It," *Straight to Hell*, issue 17 (1975).

—— "Unfit to Print," *Straight to Hell*, issue 27 (1975).

—— "It's a Sin to Tell a Lie," *Straight to Hell*, issue 37 (1977).

—— "Subscriber Wears Tasteful Jock Straps," *Straight to Hell*, issue 38 (1977).

—— "An Ideal Homosexual," *Straight to Hell*, issue 42 (1978).

—— "Wax Fruit," *Straight to Hell*, issue 48 (1980).

—— *Meat: True Homosexual Experiences from STH.* Introduction by Charles Shively. (San Francisco: Gay Sunshine Press, 1981).

—— *Flesh: True Homosexual Experiences from STH, Volume 2.* Introduction by John Mitzel. (San Francisco: Gay Sunshine Press, 1982).

—— *Sex: True Homosexual Experiences from STH Writers, Volume 3.* (San Francisco: Gay Sunshine Press, 1982).

—— "*STH* Supplement," *Fag Rag Twelfth Anniversary Issue.* (Boston: Fag Rag, 1982).

—— *Cum: True Homosexual Experiences from STH Writers, Volume 4.* (San Francisco: Gay Sunshine Press, 1983).

—— *Smut: An STH Chap Book, True Homosexual Experiences from STH Writers, Volume 5.* Introduction by John Mitzel. (New York: Gay Presses of New York, 1984).

—— *Juice: True Homosexual Experiences from STH Writers, Volume 5.* (San Francisco: Gay Sunshine Press, 1984). [This volume and the two subsequent ones in the series are numbered incorrectly, because Gay Sunshine Press refused or neglected to acknowledge *Smut*.]

—— *Cruising the Movies: A Sexual Guide to "Oldies" on TV.* (New York: Gay Presses of New York, 1985). [Second edition (Los Angeles: Semiotext(e), 2015) includes uncollected installments of the "Great Moments in Movies" column that appeared in *Christopher Street*, issues 74 (1983); 94 (1984); 96, 98, 99, 100, 101 (1985); 102, 103, 104, 106 (1986); and 107 (1987).]

—— *Wads: True Homosexual Experiences from STH Writers, Volume 6.* (San Francisco: Gay Sunshine Press, 1985).

—— "Sex" and "News Hawk" columns, *New York Native*, February 17– November 17, 1986.

—— "Art from the Post-Heterosexual Age," *Art & Text*, no. 20 (February–April 1986).

—— *Cream: True Homosexual Experiences from STH Writers, Volume 7.* (San Francisco: Gay Sunshine Press, 1986).

—— *Filth: An STH Chap Book.* (New York: Gay Presses of New York, 1987).

—— *Skin: True Homosexual Experiences from STH Writers.* Introduction by Harold Norse. (San Francisco: Bright Tyger Press, 1988). [In colophon: *Homosexual Experiences from the Classical Period, 1940–1980.*]

—— *Raunch: True Homosexual Experiences from STH, Volume 11.* Introduction by French Wall. (Boston: Fidelity Publishing, 1990).

—— "So, Long Sucker," manuscript, circa 1990. Boyd McDonald Papers, Collection Number: 7782. Cornell University Library, Division of Rare and Manuscript Collections, Human Sexuality Collection.

—— *Lewd: True Homosexual Experiences from STH, Volume 12.* Introduction by Bill Andriette. (Boston: Fidelity Publishing, 1992).

—— *Scum: True Homosexual Experiences. An STH Chapbook, Volume 13.* Introduction by Edward T. Hougen. (Boston: Fidelity Publishing, 1993).

Mark McDonald, "Don't Judge Talent Merely by Sex," (letter to the Sports Editor), *New York Times*, May 25, 1975.

John McPhee, "Omission," *The New Yorker*, September 14, 2015.

Billy Miller, "The Wonderful, Sexual World of Bob Mizer," *Huffington Post*, November 10, 2013.

John Mitzel, "A Sex-Revved Thoreau," *The Guide* (Boston), vol. 13, no. 11 (November 1993).

John Mitzel and Steven Abbott, *Myra and Gore: A New View of* Myra Breckinridge *and a Candid Interview with Gore Vidal.* (Dorchester, MA: Manifest Destiny Books, 1974).

Bill Morgan and Nancy J. Peters, Howl *on Trial: The Battle for Free Expression.* (San Francisco: City Lights Books, 2006).

Motion Picture Producers and Distributors of America, "The Motion Picture Production Code of 1930," *www.artsreformation.com/a001/hays-code.html.*

Kliph Nesteroff, "Whatever Became Of... Richard Lamparski?" *http://blog. wfmu.org*, March 25, 2007.

Harold Norse Papers, BANC MSS 2010/172, The Bancroft Library, University of California, Berkeley. [Letters from Boyd McDonald to Norse are dated April 19 and 26, and May 12, 1987; May 17, 1990.]

"Obituary: Dorothy J. Shortway," *Courier-News* (Bridgewater, NJ), March 21, 2003.

"Obituary: Mark McDonald, Essex Resident," *Hartford Courant*, March 15, 2002.

"Obituary: Robert Boerth," *Hartford Courant*, February 9, 2002.

"Obituary: Verle B. McDonald," *Orange County Register*, February 16, 2006.

Jeff Perrotti, "Video Interview with Boyd McDonald," conducted April 3, 1989. William Andriette Papers, Collection Number: 7725. Cornell University Library, Division of Rare and Manuscript Collections, Human Sexuality Collection.

Felice Picano, *Art and Sex in Greenwich Village.* (New York: Carroll & Graf, 2007).

Harry Alan Potamkin, "Film Cults," in *The Compound Cinema.* (New York: Teachers College Press, 1977).

John Preston, "Roll Call: *Straight to Hell*," *Numbers*, vol. 20 (October 1979).

"Provence Antiques," (advertisement) in *The International Antiques Yearbook 1973.* (London: Studio Vista Limited, 1973).

Manuel Puig, *Kiss of the Spider Woman*. Translated by Thomas Colchie. (New York: Alfred A. Knopf, 1979).

Manuel Puig and Ronald Christ, "A Last Interview with Manuel Puig," *World Literature Today*, vol. 65, no. 4 (Autumn 1991).

"Red Visitors Cause Rumpus," *Life*, April 4, 1949.

Matthew Rettenmund, "Whatever Became Of... Richard Lamparski?: An Exclusive Interview with Mr. Yesterday," *www.boyculture.com*, October 23, 2012.

Rex, *Speeding: The Old Reliable Photos of David Hurles*. (San Francisco: Green Candy Press, 2005).

David S. Reynolds, *Walt Whitman's America: A Cultural Biography*. (New York: Knopf, 1995).

Richard Halworth Rovere, *Senator Joe McCarthy*. (Berkeley: University of California Press, 1959).

Andrew Sarris, *The American Cinema: Directors and Directions, 1929–1968*. (New York: Dutton, 1968).

"Schine at Harvard: Boy with the Baton," *Harvard Crimson*, May 7, 1954.

A Scum Crazy Kid, "Rough Trade," *Straight to Hell*, issue 13 (1974).

Shirley Sealey, *Celebrity Sex Register*. (New York: Simon and Schuster, 1982).

Douglass Shand-Tucci, *The Crimson Letter: Harvard, Homosexuality, and the Shaping of American Culture*. (New York: St. Martin's Press, 2003).

Charles Shively, "*Fag Rag*: The Most Loathsome Publication in the English Language," *http://homoencyclopedia.com/wap/pdf/fagrag-scans.pdf*. Manuscript, early 1990s.

——— "Don't Mourn, Sodomize!" *The Guide* (Boston), vol. 13, no. 11 (November 1993).

B. F. Skinner, *About Behaviorism*. (New York: Vintage, 1976).

Stephanie D. Smith, "Obituary: Richard Shortway, Former Condé Nast Exec," *Women's Wear Daily*, November 12, 2008.

Susan Sontag, "Notes on 'Camp'" in *Against Interpretation and Other Essays*. (New York: Farrar, Straus and Giroux, 1966).

Justin Spring, *Secret Historian: The Life and Times of Samuel Steward, Professor, Tattoo Artist, and Sexual Renegade*. (New York: Farrar, Straus and Giroux, 2010).

Samuel Steward (as John McAndrews), "The Male Homosexual and Marriage," *Der Kreis*, vol. 29 (February 1961).

James Tamulis, "In Praise of Jockey Shorts," *Christopher Street*, issue 82 (November 1983).

Ben Thayer, "Farewell to a 'Venerable' Radical Gay Magazine," *www.williamapercy.com*, May 6, 2010.

"Theodore Morrison, Poet and Professor, 87," *New York Times*, November 29, 1988.

Colm Tóibín, *Love in a Dark Time*. (New York: Scribner, 2002).

Kenneth Tynan, "The Girl in the Black Helmet," *The New Yorker*, June 11, 1979.

"U. S. Editions of *Leaves of Grass*," *www.whitmanarchive.org*.

Brian Van der Horst, "Straight to Hell," *Village Voice*, August 29, 1974.

Robert Vanderlan, *Intellectuals Incorporated: Politics, Art, and Ideas Inside Henry Luce's Media Empire*. (Philadelphia: University of Pennsylvania Press, 2010).

Gore Vidal, *The City and the Pillar*. (New York: E. P. Dutton, 1948).

—— *Myra Breckinridge*. (New York: Little, Brown, 1968).

—— "Some Memories of the Glorious Bird and an Earlier Self," in *United States: Essays 1952–1992*. (New York: Random House, 1993).

Dan Wakefield, "All Boys Aren't Athletes, and Some Survive," *New York Times*, May 11, 1975.

John Waters, "Outsider Porn," in *Role Models*. (New York: Farrar, Straus and Giroux, 2010).

Victor Weaver, "Sex Speaks," *Straight to Hell*, issue 53 (1983).

Bernard Welt, "One Man's Meat," in *Mythomania: Fantasies, Fables and Sheer Lies in Contemporary American Popular Culture*. (Los Angeles: Art issues. Press, 1996).

Walt Whitman, *Leaves of Grass*. First edition. (Brooklyn, NY, 1855). [The poem "I Am He That Aches with Love" first appeared in the 1867 edition of *Leaves of Grass*.]

William H. Whyte, *The Essential William H. Whyte*. Edited by Albert LaFarge. (New York: Fordham University Press, 2000).

—— *The Organization Man*. (Philadelphia: University of Pennsylvania Press, 2002).

Hans J. Wollstein, *Vixens, Floozies and Molls: 28 Actresses of the Late 1920s and 1930s Hollywood*. (Jefferson, NC: McFarland & Company, 1999).

Anthony à Wood, *Athenæ Oxonienses: an exact history of all the writers and bishops who have had their education in the University of Oxford from 1500 to 1690, to which are added the Fasti, or Annals of the said University for the said time*. (London: 1691–1692, 2 vols. folio).

Reed Woodhouse, *Unlimited Embrace: A Canon of Gay Fiction, 1945–1995*. (Amherst: University of Massachusetts Press, 2000).

"X-Rated Film Closes Cinematheque," *Terrapin*. (Yearbook, University of Maryland at College Park, Class of 1979).

Acknowledgments

Parts of this book were previously published as the introduction to *Cruising the Movies: A Sexual Guide to "Oldies" on TV* (Los Angeles: Semiotext(e), 2015); and as "The Streets Are My Cinema," *Little Joe*, no. 5 (2015).

All images courtesy of ONE National Gay and Lesbian Archives, except the following: collection of the author, pp. 17, 19, 26, 43, 128, 131, 156, 160, 168, 191; Cornell University Library (photographed by Bernard Yenelouis), pp. 5, 22, 79; Gay Presses of New York, pp. 145, 169; Brenda Hahn, p. 58; James Hamilton, p. 85; Merry Laporta, p. 35; Library of Congress, Farm Security Administration/Office of War Information Collection, pp. 37, 39.

In *Cruising the Movies*, Boyd McDonald pays tribute to his favorite actors with "When Words Fail," a simple list of names separated by full stops and arranged alphabetically. I have composed my own alphabetical lists in acknowledging those who helped me research and write this book. I am grateful for prompt and generous responses from the following people I approached with inquiries about Boyd's life: Vince Aletti, Bill Arning, John Ashbery, Mary Corliss, Bruce Eves, Stephen Greco, Catherine Shortway McMullen, Billy Miller, Joseph Modica, Felice Picano, Charles Shively, Tom Steele, and Jim Tamulis.

As always, I thank Mark Flores, who with humor and affection has endured my many moods while writing. I could not conduct an extensive interview with David Hurles, who has been living in a nursing home in Hollywood since he had a stroke several years ago, but his pioneering example and good spirits in the face of adversity inspired much of what I have written. Jarett Kobek deserves special mention for setting aside his own writing projects to do exhaustive research about the McDonald family. I owe a great debt of gratitude to Merry Laporta, who made copies of Boyd's early articles and letters to family members available to me, and who gave her account of Boyd as a loving uncle. Bernard Yenelouis devoted a number of days of his artist's residency in Ithaca, New York, to investigating the Boyd McDonald Papers.

Thanks to Thom Andersen, Sam Ashby, Rick Bahto, Rita Belda, Michael Bronski, Caroline Byrne, Christine Chang, Durk Dehner, Julia Devine, Robbie Dewhurst, Hedi El Kholti, Eddy Falconer, Richard Fletcher, Gabriel Flores, Brenda Hahn, Bruce Hainley, James Hamilton, Dian Hanson, Richard Hawkins, Andrew Holleran, Bill Horrigan, Larry Johnson, Colby Keller, Darin Klein, David Kordansky, Stuart Krimko, Brenda Marston, James McCourt, Chuck Mobley, Michael Oliveira, Anand Pandya, Drew Sawyer, Margie Schnibbe, Jason Simon, Dean Smith, Peter Sotos, Grey Space, Bud Thomas, John Waters, and Toby Webster.

I took the return of Olga Soto, who hectors passengers on the Metro Red Line with religious messages in a combination of Aramaic, English, and Spanish, as an omen—of what I am unsure. She vanished after predicting the end of the world on 07/07/07 and reappeared eight years later, almost to the day, while I was finishing this manuscript.

There were also missed opportunities; three men who knew Boyd died only a few years before the writing of this book: *in memoriam* Larry Mitchell (1939–2012), John Mitzel (1948–2013), and Gore Vidal (1925–2012).